Cha

By
Thomas Carlyle

ANODOS BOOKS
Candida Casa

Thomas Carlyle (1795-1881)
Originally published in 1840
Editing, cover, and internal design by Alisdair MacNoravaich for Anodos Books.
Copyright © 2017 Anodos Books. All rights reserved.
Anodos Books
1c Kings Road
Whithorn
Newton Stewart
Dumfries & Galloway
DG8 8PP

Contents

CHAPTER I.	1
CHAPTER II.	7
CHAPTER III.	11
CHAPTER IV.	17
CHAPTER V.	25
CHAPTER VI.	35
CHAPTER VII.	45
CHAPTER VIII.	49
CHAPTER IX.	63
CHAPTER X.	69

CHAPTER I.

CONDITION OF ENGLAND QUESTION

A FEELING very generally exists that the condition and disposition of the Working Classes is a rather ominous matter at present; that something ought to be said, something ought to be done, in regard to it. And surely, at an epoch of history when the 'National Petition' carts itself in waggons along the streets, and is presented 'bound with iron hoops, four men bearing it', to a Reformed House of Commons; and Chartism numbered by the million and half, taking nothing by its iron-hooped Petition, breaks out into brickbats, cheap pikes, and even into sputterings of conflagration, such very general feeling cannot be considered unnatural! To us individually this matter appears, and has for many years appeared, to be the most ominous of all practical matters whatever; a matter in regard to which if something be not done, something will *do* itself one day, and in a fashion that will please nobody. The time is verily come for acting in it; how much more for consultation about acting in it, for speech and articulate inquiry about it!

We are aware that, according to the newspapers, Chartism is extinct; that a Reform Ministry has 'put down the chimera of Chartism' in the most felicitous effectual manner. So say the newspapers;—and yet, alas, most readers of newspapers know withal that it is indeed the 'chimera' of Chartism, not the reality, which has been put down. The distracted incoherent embodiment of Chartism, whereby in late months it took shape and became visible, this has been put down; or rather has fallen down and gone asunder by gravitation and law of nature; but the living essence of Chartism has not been put down. Chartism means the bitter discontent grown fierce and mad, the wrong condition therefore or the wrong disposition, of the Working Classes of England. It is a new name for a thing which has had many names, which will yet have many. The matter of Chartism is weighty, deep-rooted, far-extending; did not begin yesterday; will by no means end this day or to-morrow. Reform Ministry, constabulary rural police, new levy of soldiers, grants of money to Birmingham; all this is well, or is not well; all this will put down only the embodiment or 'chimera' of Chartism. The essence continuing, new and ever new embodiments, chimeras madder or less mad, have to continue. The melancholy fact remains, that this thing known at present by the name Chartism does exist; has existed; and, either 'put down,' into secret treason, with rusty pistols, vitriol-bottle and match-box, or openly brandishing pike and torch (one knows not in which case *more* fatal-looking), is like to exist till quite other methods have been tried with it. What means this bitter discontent of the Working Classes? Whence comes it, whither goes it? Above all, at what price, on what terms, will it probably consent to depart from us and die into rest? These are questions.

To say that it is mad, incendiary, nefarious, is no answer. To say all this, in never so many dialects, is saying little. 'Glasgow Thuggery,' 'Glasgow Thugs;' it is a witty nickname: the practice of 'Number 60' entering his dark room, to contract for and settle the price of blood with operative assassins, in a Christian city, once distinguished by its rigorous Christianism, is doubtless a fact worthy of all horror; but what will horror do for it? What will execration; nay at bottom, what will condemnation and banishment to Botany Bay do for it? Glasgow Thuggery, Chartist torch-meetings, Birmingham riots, Swing conflagrations, are so many symptoms on the surface; you abolish the symptom to no purpose, if the disease is left untouched. Boils on the surface are curable or incurable,—small matter which, while the virulent humour festers deep within; poisoning the sources of life; and certain enough to find for itself ever new boils and sore issues; ways of announcing that it continues there, that it would fain not continue there.

Delirious Chartism will not have raged entirely to no purpose, as indeed no earthly thing does so, if it have forced all thinking men of the community to think of this vital matter, too apt to be overlooked otherwise. Is the condition of the English working people wrong; so wrong that rational working men cannot, will not, and even should not rest quiet under it? A most grave case, complex beyond all others in the world; a case wherein Botany Bay, constabulary rural police, and such like, will avail but little. Or is the discontent itself mad, like the shape it took? Not the condition of the working people that is wrong; but their disposition, their own thoughts, beliefs and feelings that are wrong? This too were a most grave case, little less alarming, little less complex than the former one. In this case too, where constabulary police and mere rigour of coercion seems more at home, coercion will by no means do all, coercion by itself will not even do much. If there do exist general madness of discontent, then sanity and some measure of content must be brought about again,—not by constabulary police alone. When the thoughts of a people, in the great mass of it, have grown mad, the combined issue of that people's workings will be a madness, an incoherency and ruin! Sanity will have to be recovered for the general mass; coercion itself will otherwise cease to be able to coerce.

We have heard it asked, Why Parliament throws no light on this question of the Working Classes, and the condition or disposition they are in? Truly to a remote observer of Parliamentary procedure it seems surprising, especially in late Reformed times, to see what space this question occupies in the Debates of the Nation. Can any other business whatsoever be so pressing on legislators? A Reformed Parliament, one would think, should inquire into popular discontents before they get the length of pikes and torches! For what end at all are men, Honourable Members and Reform Members, sent to St. Stephen's, with clamour and effort; kept talking, struggling, motioning and counter-motioning? The condition of the great body of people in a country is the condition of the country itself: this you would say is a truism in all times; a truism rather pressing to get recognised as a truth now, and be acted upon, in these times. Yet read Hansard's Debates, or the Morning Papers, if you have nothing to do! The old grand question, whether A is to be in office or B, with the innumerable subsidiary questions growing out of that, courting paragraphs and suffrages for a blessed solution of that: Canada question, Irish Appropriation question, West India question. Queen's Bedchamber question; Game Laws, Usury Laws; African Blacks, Hill Coolies, Smithfield cattle, and Dog-carts,—all manner of questions and subjects, except simply this the alpha and omega of all! Surely Honourable Members ought to speak of the Condition-of-England question too. Radical Members, above all; friends of the people; chosen with effort, by the people, to interpret and articulate the dumb deep want of the people! To a remote observer they seem oblivious of their duty. Are they not there, by trade, mission, and express appointment of themselves and others, to speak for the good of the British Nation? Whatsoever great British interest can the least speak for itself, for that beyond all they are called to speak. They are either speakers for that great dumb toiling class which cannot speak, or they are nothing that one can well specify.

Alas, the remote observer knows not the nature of Parliaments: how Parliaments, extant there for the British Nation's sake, find that they are extant withal for their own sake; how Parliaments travel so naturally in their deep-rutted routine, common-place worn into ruts axle-deep, from which only strength, insight and courageous generous exertion can lift any Parliament or vehicle; how in Parliaments, Reformed or Unreformed, there may chance to be a strong man, an original, clear-sighted, great-hearted, patient and valiant man, or to be none such;—how, on the whole, Parliaments, lumbering along in their deep ruts of commonplace, find, as so many of us otherwise do, that the ruts are axle-deep, and the travelling very toilsome of itself, and for the day the evil thereof sufficient! What Parliaments ought to have done in this business, what they will, can or cannot yet do, and where the limits of their faculty and culpability may lie, in regard to it, were a long investigation; into which we need not enter at this moment. What they have done is unhappily plain enough. Hitherto, on this most national of questions, the Collective Wisdom of the Nation has availed us as good as nothing whatever.

And yet, as we say, it is a question which cannot be left to the Collective Folly of the Nation! In or out of Parliament, darkness, neglect, hallucination must contrive to cease in regard to it; true insight into it must be had. How inexpressibly useful were true insight into it; a genuine understanding by the upper classes of society what it is that the under classes intrinsically mean; a clear interpretation of the thought which at heart torments these wild inarticulate souls, struggling there, with inarticulate uproar, like dumb creatures in pain, unable to speak what is in them! Something they do mean; some true thing withal, in the centre of their confused hearts,—for they are hearts created by Heaven too: to the Heaven it is clear what thing; to us not clear. Would that it were! Perfect clearness on it were equivalent to remedy of it. For, as is well said, all battle is misunderstanding; did the parties know one another, the battle would cease. No man at bottom means injustice; it is always for some obscure distorted image of a right that he contends: an obscure image diffracted, exaggerated, in the wonderfullest way, by natural dimness and selfishness; getting tenfold more diffracted by exasperation of contest, till at length it become all but irrecognisable; yet still the image of a right. Could a man own to himself that the thing he fought for was wrong, contrary to fairness and the law of reason, he would own also that it thereby stood condemned and hopeless; he could fight for it no longer. Nay independently of right, could the contending parties get but accurately to discern one another's might and strength to contend, the one would peaceably yield to the other and to Necessity; the contest in this case too were over. No African expedition now, as in the days of Herodotus, is fitted out *against the South-wind*. One expedition was satisfactory in that department. The South-wind Simoom continues blowing occasionally, hateful as ever, maddening as ever; but one expedition was enough. Do we not all submit to Death? The highest sentence of the law, sentence of death, is passed on all of us by the fact of birth; yet we live patiently under it, patiently undergo it when the hour comes. Clear undeniable right, clear undeniable might: either of these once ascertained puts an end to battle. All battle is a confused experiment to ascertain one and both of these.

What are the rights, what are the mights of the discontented Working Classes in England at this epoch? He were an Œdipus, and deliverer from sad social pestilence, who could resolve us fully! For we may say beforehand, The struggle that divides the upper and lower in society over Europe, and more painfully and notably in England than elsewhere, this too is a struggle which will end and adjust itself as all other struggles do and have done, by making the right clear and the might clear; not otherwise than by that. Meantime, the questions. Why are the Working Classes discontented; what is their condition, economical, moral, in their houses and their hearts, as it is in reality and as they figure it to themselves to be; what do they complain of; what ought they, and ought they not to complain of?—these are measurable questions; on some of these any common mortal, did he but turn his eyes to them, might throw some light. Certain researches and considerations of ours on the matter, since no one else will undertake it, are now to be made public. The researches have yielded us little, almost nothing; but the considerations are of old date, and press to have utterance. We are not without hope that our general notion of the business, if we can get it uttered at all, will meet some assent from many candid men.

CHAPTER II.
STATISICS

A WITTY statesman said you might prove anything by figures. We have looked into various statistic works, Statistic-Society Reports, Poor-Law Reports, Reports and Pamphlets not a few, with a sedulous eye to this question of the Working Classes and their general condition in England; we grieve to say, with as good as no result whatever. Assertion swallows assertion; according to the old Proverb, 'as the *statist* thinks, the bell clinks!' Tables are like cobwebs, like the sieve of the Danaides; beautifully reticulated, orderly to look upon, but which will hold no conclusion. Tables are abstractions, and the object a most concrete one, so difficult to read the essence of. There are innumerable circumstances; and one circumstance left out may be the vital one on which all turned. Statistics is a science which ought to be honourable, the basis of many most important sciences; but it is not to be carried on by steam, this science, any more than others are; a wise head is requisite for carrying it on. Conclusive facts are inseparable from inconclusive except by a head that already understands and knows. Vain to send the purblind and blind to the shore of a Pactolus never so golden: these find only gravel; the seer and finder alone picks up gold grains there. And now the purblind offering you, with asseveration and protrusive importunity, his basket of gravel as gold, what steps are to be taken with him?— Statistics, one may hope, will improve gradually, and become good for something. Meanwhile it is to be feared, the crabbed satirist was partly right, as things go: 'A judicious man, says he, 'looks at Statistics, not to get knowledge, but to save himself from having ignorance foisted on him.' With what serene conclusiveness a member of some Useful-Knowledge Society stops your mouth with a figure of arithmetic! To him it seems he has there extracted the elixir of the matter, on which now nothing more can be said. It is needful that you look into his said extracted elixir; and ascertain, alas, too probably, not without a sigh, that it is wash and vapidity, good only for the gutters.

Twice or three times have we heard the lamentations and prophecies of a humane Jeremiah, mourner for the poor, cut short by a statistic fact of the most decisive nature: How can the condition of the poor be other than good, be other than better; has not the average duration of life in England, and therefore among the most numerous class in England, been proved to have increased? Our Jeremiah had to admit that, if so, it was an astounding fact; whereby all that ever he, for his part, had observed on other sides of the matter was overset without remedy. If life last longer, life must be less worn upon, by outward suffering, by inward discontent, by hardship of any kind; the general condition of the poor must be bettering instead of worsening. So was our Jeremiah cut short. And now for the 'proof'? Readers who are curious in statistic proofs may see it drawn out with all solemnity, in a Pamphlet 'published by Charles Knight and Company,'[1]—and perhaps himself draw inferences from it. Northampton Tables, compiled by Dr. Price 'from registers of the Parish of All Saints from 1735 to 1780;' Carlisle Tables, collected by Dr. Heysham from observation of Carlisle City for eight years, 'the calculations founded on them' conducted by another Doctor; incredible 'document considered satisfactory by men of science in France:'—alas, is it not as if some zealous scientific son of Adam had proved the deepening of the Ocean, by survey, accurate or cursory, of two mud-plashes on the coast of the Isle of Dogs? 'Not to get knowledge, but to save yourself from having ignorance foisted on you!'

The condition of the working man in this country, what it is and has been, whether it is improving or retrograding,—is a question to which from statistics hitherto no solution can be got. Hitherto, after many tables and statements, one is still left mainly to what he can ascertain by his own eyes, looking at the concrete phenomenon for himself. There is no other method; and yet it is a most imperfect method. Each man expands his own handbreadth of observation to the limits of the general whole; more or less, each man must take what he himself has seen and ascertained for a sample of all that is seeable and ascertainable. Hence discrepancies, controversies, wide-spread, long-continued; which there is at present no means or hope of satisfactorily ending. When Parliament takes up 'the Condition-of-England question,' as it will have to do one day, then indeed much may be amended! Inquiries wisely gone into, even on this most complex matter, will

---

[1] An Essay on the Means of Insurance against the Casualties of &c. &c. London, Charles Knight and Company, 1836. Price two shillings.

yield results worth something, not nothing. But it is a most complex matter; on which, whether for the past or the present, Statistic Inquiry, with its limited means, with its short vision and headlong extensive dogmatism, as yet too often throws not light, but error worse than darkness.

What constitutes the well-being of a man? Many things ; of which the wages he gets, and the bread he buys with them, are but one preliminary item. Grant, however, that the wages were the whole; that once knowing the wages and the price of bread, we know all; then what are the wages? Statistic Inquiry, in its present unguided condition, cannot tell. The average rate of day's wages is not correctly ascertained for any portion of this country; not only not for half-centuries, it is not even ascertained anywhere for decades or years: far from instituting comparisons with the past, the present itself is unknown to us. And then, given the average of wages, what is the constancy of employment; what is the difficulty of finding employment; the fluctuation from season to season, from year to year? Is it constant, calculable wages; or fluctuating, incalculable, more or less of the nature of gambling? This secondary circumstance, of quality in wages, is perhaps even more important than the primary one of quantity. Farther we ask, Can the labourer, by thrift and industry, hope to rise to mastership; or is such hope cut off from him ? How is he related to his employer; by bonds of friendliness and mutual help; or by hostility, opposition, and chains of mutual necessity alone? In a word, what degree of contentment can a human creature be supposed to enjoy in that position? With hunger preying on him, his contentment is likely to be small! But even with abundance, his discontent, his real misery may be great. The labourer's feelings, his notion of being justly dealt with or unjustly; his wholesome composure, frugality, prosperity in the one case, his acrid unrest, recklessness, gin-drinking, and gradual ruin in the other,—how shall figures of arithmetic represent all this? So much is still to be ascertained; much of it by no means easy to ascertain! Till, among the 'Hill Cooly' and 'Dog-cart' questions, there arise in Parliament and extensively out of it a 'Condition-of-England question,' and quite a new set of inquirers and methods, little of it is likely to be ascertained.

One fact on this subject, a fact which arithmetic *is* capable of representing, we have often considered would be worth all the rest: Whether the labourer, whatever his wages are, is saving money? Laying up money, he proves that his condition, painful as it may be without and within, is not yet desperate; that he looks forward to a better day coming, and is still resolutely steering towards the same; that all the lights and darknesses of his lot are united under a blessed radiance of hope,—the last, first, nay one may say the sole blessedness of man. Is the habit of saving increased and increasing, or the contrary? Where the present writer has been able to look with his own eyes, it is decreasing, and in many quarters all but disappearing. Statistic science turns up her Savings-Bank Accounts, and answers, "Increasing rapidly." Would that one could believe it! But the Danaides'-sieve character of such statistic reticulated documents is too manifest. A few years ago, in regions where thrift, to one's own knowledge, still was, Savings-Banks were not; the labourer lent his money to some farmer, of capital, or supposed to be of capital,—and has too often lost it since; or he bought a cow with it, bought a cottage with it; nay hid it under his thatch: the Savings-Banks books then exhibited mere blank and zero. That they swell yearly now, if such be the fact, indicates that what thrift exists does gradually resort more and more thither rather than elsewhither; but the question, Is thrift increasing? runs through the reticulation, and is as water spilt on the ground, not to be gathered here.

These are inquiries on which, had there been a proper 'Condition-of-England question,' some light would have been thrown, before 'torch-meetings' arose to illustrate them! Far as they lie out of the course of Parliamentary routine, they should have been gone into, should have been glanced at, in one or the other fashion. A Legislature making laws for the Working Classes, in total uncertainty as to these things, is legislating in the dark; not wisely, nor to good issues. The simple fundamental question, Can the labouring man in this England of ours, who is willing to labour, find work, and subsistence by his work? is matter of mere conjecture and assertion hitherto; not ascertainable by authentic evidence: the Legislature, satisfied to legislate in the dark, has not yet sought any evidence on it. They pass their New Poor-Law Bill, without evidence as to all this. Perhaps their New Poor-Law Bill is itself only intended as an *experimentum crucis* to ascertain all this? Chartism is an answer, seemingly not in the affirmative.

CHAPTER III.

NEW POOR-LAW

To read the Reports of the Poor-Law Commissioners, if one had faith enough, would be a pleasure to the friend of humanity. One sole recipe seems to have been needful for the woes of England: 'refusal of out-door relief.' England lay in sick discontent, writhing powerless on its fever-bed, dark, nigh, desperate, in wastefulness, want, improvidence, and eating care, till like Hyperion down the eastern steeps, the Poor-Law Commissioners arose, and said, Let there be workhouses, and bread of affliction and water of affliction there! It was a simple invention; as all truly great inventions are. And see, in any quarter, instantly as the walls of the workhouse arise, misery and necessity fly away, out of sight, —out of being, as is fondly hoped, and dissolve into the inane; industry, frugality, fertility, rise of wages, peace on earth and goodwill towards men do,—in the Poor-Law Commissioners' Reports,—infallibly, rapidly or not so rapidly, to the joy of all parties, supervene. It was a consummation devoutly to be wished. We have looked over these four annual Poor-Law Reports with a variety of reflections; with no thought that our Poor-Law Commissioners are the inhuman men their enemies accuse them of being; with a feeling of thankfulness rather that there do exist men of that structure too; with a persuasion deeper and deeper that Nature, who makes nothing to no purpose, has not made either them or their Poor-Law Amendment Act in vain. We hope to prove that they and it were an indispensable element, harsh but salutary, in the progress of things.

That this Poor-Law Amendment Act meanwhile should be, as we sometimes hear it named, the 'chief glory' of a Reform Cabinet, betokens, one would imagine, rather a scarcity of glory there. To say to the poor, Ye shall eat the bread of affliction and drink the water of affliction, and be very miserable while here, required not so much a stretch of heroic faculty in any sense, as due toughness of bowels. If paupers are made miserable, paupers will needs decline in multitude. It is a secret known to all rat-catchers: stop up the granary-crevices, afflict with continual mewing, alarm, and going-off of traps, your 'chargeable labourers' disappear, and cease from the establishment. A still briefer method is that of arsenic;

perhaps even a milder, where otherwise permissible. Rats and paupers can be abolished; the human faculty was from of old adequate to grind them down, slowly or at once, and needed no ghost or Reform Ministry to teach it. Furthermore when one hears of 'all the labour of the country being absorbed into employment' by this new system of affliction, when labour complaining of want can find no audience, one cannot but pause. That misery and unemployed labour should 'disappear' in that case is natural enough; should go out of sight,—but out of existence? What we do know is that 'the rates are diminished,' as they cannot well help being; that no statistic tables as yet report much increase of deaths by starvation: this we do know, and not veryconclusively anything more than this. If this be absorption of all the labour of the country, then all the labour of the country is absorbed.

To believe practically that the poor and luckless are here only as a nuisance to be abraded and abated, and in some permissible manner made away with, and swept out of sight, is not an amiable faith. That the arrangements of good and ill success in this perplexed scramble of a world, which a blind goddess was always thought to preside over, are in fact the work of a seeing goddess or god, and require only not to be meddled with: what stretch of heroic faculty or inspiration of genius was needed to teach one that? To button your pockets and stand still, is no complex recipe. *Laissez faire, laissez passer!* Whatever goes on, ought it not to go on; 'the widow picking nettles for her children's dinner, and the perfumed seigneur delicately lounging in the Œil-du-Bœuf, who has an alchemy whereby he will extract from her the third nettle, and name it rent and law?' What is written and enacted, has it not black-on-white to shew for itself? Justice is justice; but all attorney's parchment is of the nature of Targum or sacred-parchment. In brief, ours is a world requiring only to be well let alone. Scramble along, thou insane scramble of a world, with thy pope's tiaras, king's mantles and beggar's gabardines, chivalry-ribbons and plebeian gallows-ropes, where a Paul shall die on the gibbet and a Nero sit fiddling as imperial Caesar; *thou* art all right, and shalt scramble even so; and whoever in the press is trodden down, has only to lie there and be trampled broad:—Such at bottom seems to be the chief social principle, if principle it have, which the Poor-Law Amendment Act has the merit of courageously asserting, in opposition to many things. A chief social principle which this present writer, for one, will by no manner of means believe in, but pronounce at all fit times to be false, heretical and damnable, if ever aught was!

And yet, as we said, Nature makes nothing in vain; not even a Poor-Law Amendment Act. For withal we are far from joining in the outcry raised against these poor Poor-Law Commissioners, as if they were tigers in men's shape; as if their Amendment Act were a mere monstrosity and horror, deserving instant abrogation. They are not tigers; they are men filled with an idea of a theory: their Amendment Act, heretical and damnable as a whole truth, is orthodox laudable as a *half*-truth; and was imperatively required to be put in practice. To create men filled with a theory that refusal of out-door relief was the one thing needful: Nature had no readier way of getting out-door relief refused. In fact, if we look at the old Poor-Law, in its assertion of the opposite social principle, that Fortune's awards are *not* those of Justice, we shall find it to have become still more unsupportable, demanding, if England was not destined for speedy anarchy, to be done away with.

Any law, however well meant as a law, which has become a bounty on unthrift, idleness, bastardy and beer-drinking, must be put an end to. In all ways it needs, especially in these times, to be proclaimed aloud that for the idle man there is no place in this England of ours. He that will not work, and save according to his means, let him go elsewhither; let him know that for *him* the Law has made no soft provision, but a hard and stern one; that by the Law of Nature, which the Law of England would vainly contend against in the long-run, *he* is doomed either to quit these habits, or miserably be extruded from this Earth, which is made on principles different from these. He that will not work according to his faculty, let him perish according to his necessity: there is no law juster than that. Would to heaven one could preach it abroad into the hearts of all sons and daughters of Adam, for it is a law applicable to all; and bring it to bear, with practical obligation strict as the Poor-Law Bastille, on all! We had then, in good truth, a 'perfect constitution of society;' and 'God's fair earth and Task-garden, where whosoever is not working must be begging or stealing,' were then actually what always, through so many changes and struggles, it is endeavouring to become.

That this law of No work no recompense, should first of all be enforced on the *manual* worker, and brought stringently home to him and his numerous class, while so many other classes and persons still go loose from it, was natural to the case. Let it be enforced there, and rigidly made good;—alas, not by such simple methods as 'refusal of outdoor relief,' but by far other and costlier ones; which too, however, a bountiful Providence is not unfurnished with, nor, in these latter generations (if we will understand their convulsions and confusions), sparing to apply. Work is the mission of man in this Earth. A day is ever struggling forward, a day will arrive in some approximate degree, when he who has no work to do, by whatever name he may be named, will not find it good to shew himself in our quarter of the Solar System; but may go and look out elsewhere. If there be any *Idle* Planet discoverable?—Let the honest working man rejoice that such law, the first of Nature, has been made good on him; and hope that, by and by, all else will be made good. It is the beginning of all. We define the harsh New Poor-Law to be withal a 'protection of the thrifty labourer against the thriftless and dissolute;' a thing inexpressibly important; a *half*-result, detestable, if you will, when looked upon as the whole result; yet without which the whole result is forever unattainable. Let wastefulness, idleness, drunkenness, improvidence take the fate which God has appointed them; that their opposites may also have a chance for *their* fate. Let the Poor-Law Administrators be considered as useful labourers whom Nature has furnished with a whole theory of the universe, that they might accomplish an indispensable fractional practice there, and prosper in it in spite of much contradiction.

We will praise the New Poor-Law, farther, as the probable preliminary of *some* general charge to be taken of the lowest classes by the higher. Any general charge whatsoever, rather than a conflict of charges, varying from parish to parish; the emblem of darkness, of unreadable confusion. Supervisal by the central government, in what spirit soever executed, is supervisal from a centre. By degrees the object will become clearer, as it is at once made thereby universally conspicuous. By degrees true vision of it will become attainable, will be universally attained; whatsoever order regarding it is just and wise, as grounded on the truth of it, will then be capable of being taken. Let us welcome the New

Poor-Law as the harsh beginning of much, the harsh ending of much! Most harsh and barren lies the new ploughers' fallow-field, the crude subsoil all turned up, which never saw the sun; which as yet grows no herb; which has 'out-door relief for no one. Yet patience: innumerable weeds and corruptions lie safely turned down and extinguished under it; this same crude subsoil is the first step of all true husbandry; by Heaven's blessing and the skyey influences, fruits that are good and blessed will yet come of it.

For, in truth, the claim of the poor labourer is something quite other than that 'Statute of the Forty-third of Elizabeth' will ever fulfil for him. Not to be supported by roundsmen systems, by never so liberal parish doles, or lodged in free and easy workhouses when distress overtakes him; not for this, however in words he may clamour for it; not for this, but for something far different does the heart of him struggle. It is 'for justice' that he struggles; for 'just wages,'—not in money alone! An ever-toiling inferior, he would fain (though as yet he knows it not) find for himself a superior that should lovingly and wisely govern: is not that too the 'just wages' of his service done? It is for a manlike place and relation, in this world where he sees himself a man, that he struggles. At bottom may we not say, it is even for this, That guidance and government, which he cannot give himself, which in our so complex world he can no longer do without, might be afforded him? The thing he struggles for is one which no Forty-third of Elizabeth is in any condition to furnish him, to put him on the road towards getting. Let him quit the Forty-third of Elizabeth altogether; and rejoice that the Poor-Law Amendment Act has, even by harsh methods and against his own will, forced him away from it. That was a broken reed to lean on, if there ever was one; and did but run into his lamed right-hand. Let him cast it far from him, that broken reed, and look to quite the opposite point of the heavens for help. His unlamed right-hand, with the cunning industry that lies in it, is not this defined to be 'the sceptre of our Planet'? He that can work is a born king of something; is in communion with Nature, is master of a thing or things, is a priest and king of Nature so far. He that can work at nothing is but a usurping king, be his trappings what they may; he is the born slave of all things. Let a man honour his craftmanship, his *can-do*; and know that his rights of man have no concern at all with the Forty-third of Elizabeth.

CHAPTER IV.
FINEST PEASANTRY IN THE WORLD.

THE New Poor-Law is as announcement, sufficiently distinct, that whosoever will not work ought not to live. Can the poor man that is willing to work, always find work, and live by his work? Statistic Inquiry, as we saw, has no answer to give. Legislation presupposes the answer—to be in the affirmative. A large postulate; which should have been made a proposition of; which should have been demonstrated, made indubitable to all persons! A man willing to work, and unable to find work, is perhaps the saddest sight that Fortune's inequality exhibits under this sun. Burns expresses feelingly what thoughts it gave him: a poor man seeking *work*; seeking leave to toil that he might be fed and sheltered! That he might but be put on a level with the four-footed workers of the Planet which is his! There is not a horse willing to work but can get food and shelter in requital; a thing this two-footed worker has to seek for, to solicit occasionally in vain. He is nobody's two-footed worker; he is not even anybody's slave. And yet he is a *two-footed worker*; it is currently reported there is an immortal soul in him, sent down out of Heaven into the Earth; and one beholds him *seeking* for this!—Nay what will a wise Legislature say, if it turn out that he cannot find it; that the answer to their postulate proposition is not affirmative but negative?

There is one fact which Statistic Science has communicated, and a most astonishing one; the inference from which is pregnant as to this matter. Ireland has near seven millions of working people, the third unit of whom, it appears by Statistic Science, has not for thirty weeks each year as many third-rate potatoes as will suffice him. It is a fact perhaps the most eloquent that was ever written down in any language, at any date of the world's history. Was change and reformation needed in Ireland? Has Ireland been governed and guided in a 'wise and loving' manner? A government and guidance of white European men which has issued in perennial hunger of potatoes to the third man extant,— ought to drop a veil over its face, and walk out of court under conduct of proper officers; saying no word; expecting now of a surety sentence either to change or die. All men, we must repeat, were made by God, and have immortal souls in them. The

Sanspotatoe is of the selfsame stuff as the super-finest Lord Lieutenant. Not an individual Sanspotatoe human scarecrow but had a Life given him out of Heaven, with Eternities depending on it; for once and no second time. With Immensities in him, over him and round him; with feelings which a Shakspeare's speech would not utter; with desires illimitable as the Autocrat's of all the Russias! Him various thrice-honoured persons, things and institutions have long been teaching, long been guiding, governing: and it is to perpetual scarcity of third-rate potatoes, and to what depends thereon, that he has been taught and guided. Figure thyself, O high-minded, clear-headed, clean-burnished reader, clapt by enchantment into the torn coat and waste hunger-lair of that same root-devouring brother man!—

Social anomalies are things to be defended, things to be amended; and in all places and things, short of the Pit itself, there is some admixture of worth and good. Room for extenuation, for pity, for patience! And yet when the general result has come to the length of perennial starvation, argument, extenuating logic, pity and patience on that subject may be considered as drawing to a close. It may be considered that such arrangement of things will have to terminate. That it has all just men for its natural enemies. That all just men, of what outward colour soever in Politics or otherwise, will say: This cannot last, Heaven disowns it, Earth is against it; Ireland will be burnt into a black unpeopled field of ashes rather than this should last.—The woes of Ireland, or 'justice to Ireland,' is not the chapter we have to write at present. It is a deep matter, an abyssmal one, which no plummet of ours will sound. For the oppression has gone far farther than into the economics of Ireland; inwards to her very heart and soul. The Irish National character is degraded, disordered; till this recover itself, nothing is yet recovered. Immethodic, headlong, violent, mendacious: what can you make of the wretched Irishman? "A finer people never lived," as the Irish lady said to us; "only they have two faults, they do generally lie and steal: barring these"—! A people that knows not to speak the truth, and to act the truth, such people has departed from even the possibility of well-being. Such people works no longer on Nature and Reality; works now on Fantasm, Simulation, Nonentity; the result it arrives at is naturally not a thing but no-thing,—defect even of potatoes. Scarcity, futility, confusion, distraction must be perennial there. Such a people circulates not order but disorder, through every vein of it;—and the cure, if it is to be a cure, must begin at the heart: not in his condition only but in himself must the Patient be all changed. Poor Ireland! And yet let no true Irishman, who believes and sees all this, despair by reason of it. Cannot he too do something to withstand the unproductive falsehood, there as it lies accursed around him, and change it into truth, which is fruitful and blessed? Every mortal can and shall himself be a true man: it is a great thing, and the parent of great things;—as from a single acorn the whole earth might in the end be peopled with oaks! Every mortal can do something: this let him faithfully do, and leave with assured heart the issue to a Higher Power!

We English pay, even now, the bitter smart of long centuries of injustice to our neighbour Island. Injustice, doubt it not, abounds; or Ireland would not be miserable. The Earth is good, bountifully sends food and increase; if man's unwisdom did not intervene and forbid. It was an evil day when Strigul first meddled with that people. He could not extirpate them: could they but have agreed together, and extirpated him! Violent men there have been, and merciful; unjust rulers, and just; conflicting in a great element of violence, these five wild centuries now; and the violent and unjust have carried it, and we are come to *this*. England is guilty towards Ireland; and reaps at last, in full measure, the fruit of fifteen generations of wrong-doing.

But the thing we had to state here was our inference from that mournful fact of the third Sanspotatoe,—coupled with this other well-known fact that the Irish speak a partially intelligible dialect of English, and their fare across by steam is four-pence sterling! Crowds of miserable Irish darken all our towns. The wild Milesian features, looking false ingenuity, restlessness, unreason, misery and mockery, salute you on all highways and byways. The English coachman, as he whirls past, lashes the Milesian with his whip, curses him with his tongue; the Milesian is holding out his hat to beg. He is the sorest evil this country has to strive with. In his rags and laughing savagery, he is there to undertake all work that can be done by mere strength of hand and back; for wages that will purchase him potatoes. He needs only salt for condiment; he lodges to his mind in any pighutch or doghutch, roosts in outhouses; and wears a suit of tatters, the getting off and on of which is said to be a difficult operation, transacted only in festivals and the hightides of the calendar. The Saxon man if he cannot work on these terms, finds no work. He too may be ignorant; but he has not sunk from decent manhood to squalid apehood: he cannot continue there. American forests lie untilled across the ocean; the uncivilised Irishman, not by his strength but by the opposite of strength, drives out the Saxon native, takes possession in his room. There abides he, in his squalor and unreason, in his falsity and drunken violence, as the ready-made nucleus of degradation and disorder. Whosoever struggles, swimming with difficulty, may now find an example how the human being can exist not swimming but sunk. Let him sink; he is not the worst of men; not worse than this man. We have quarantines against pestilence; but there is no pestilence like that; and against it what quarantine is possible? It is lamentable to look upon. This soil of Britain, these Saxon men have cleared it, made it arable, fertile and a home for them; they and their fathers have done that. Under the sky there exists no force of men who with arms in their hands could drive them out of it; all force of men with arms these Saxons would seize, in their grim way, and fling (Heaven's justice and their own Saxon humour aiding them) swiftly into the sea. But behold, a force of men armed only with rags, ignorance and nakedness; and the Saxon owners, paralysed by invisible magic of paper formula, have to fly far, and hide themselves in Transatlantic forests. 'Irish repeal?' "Would to God," as Dutch William said, "*You* were King of Ireland, and could take yourself and it three thousand miles off,"—there to repeal it!

And yet these poor Celtiberian Irish brothers, what can *they* help it? They cannot stay at home, and starve. It is just and natural that they come hither as a curse to us. Alas, for them too it is not a luxury. It is not a straight or joyful way of avenging their sore wrongs this; but a most sad circuitous one. Yet a way it is, and an effectual way. The time has come when the Irish population must either be improved a little, or else exterminated. Plausible management, adapted to this hollow outcry or to that, will no longer do; it must be management grounded on sincerity and fact, to which the truth of things will respond—by an actual beginning of improvement to these wretched brother-men. In a state of perennial ultra-savage famine, in the midst of civilisation, they cannot continue. For that the Saxon British will ever submit to sink along with them to such a state, we assume as impossible.

There is in these latter, thank God, an ingenuity which is not false; a methodic spirit, of insight, of perseverant well-doing; a rationality and veracity which Nature with her truth does *not* disown;—withal there is a 'Berserkir-rage' in the heart of them, which will prefer all things, including destruction and self-destruction, to that. Let no man awaken it, this same Berserkir-rage! Deep-hidden it lies, far down in the centre, like genial central-fire, with stratum after stratum of arrangement, traditionary method, composed productiveness, all built above it, vivified and rendered fertile by it: justice, clearness, silence, perseverance, unhasting unresting diligence, hatred of disorder, hatred of injustice, which is the worst disorder, characterise this people; their inward fire we say, as all such fire should be, is hidden at the centre. Deep-hidden; but awakenable, but immeasurable;—let no man awaken it! With this strong silent people have the noisy vehement Irish now at length got common cause made. Ireland, now for the first time, in such strange circuitous way, does find itself embarked in the same boat with England, to sail together, or to sink together; the wretchedness of Ireland, slowly but inevitably, has crept over to us, and become our own wretchedness. The Irish population must get itself redressed and saved, for the sake of the English if for nothing else. Alas, that it should, on both sides, be poor toiling men that pay the smart for unruly Striguls, Henrys, Macdermots, and O'Donoghues! The strong have eaten sour grapes, and the teeth of the weak are set on edge. 'Curses,' says the Proverb, 'are like chickens, they return always *home*.'

But now on the whole, it seems to us, English Statistic Science, with floods of the finest peasantry in the world streaming in on us daily, may fold up her Danaides reticulations on this matter of the Working Classes; and conclude, what every man who will take the statistic spectacles off his nose, and look, may discern in town or country: That the condition of the lower multitude of English labourers approximates more and more to that of the Irish competing with them in all markets; that whatsoever labour, to which mere strength with little skill will suffice, is to be done, will be done not at the English price, but at an approximation to the Irish price: at a price superior as yet to the Irish, that is, superior to scarcity of third-rate potatoes for thirty weeks yearly; superior, yet hourly, with the arrival of every new steamboat, sinking nearer to an equality with that. Half-a-million handloom weavers, working fifteen hours a-day, in perpetual inability to procure thereby enough of the coarsest food; English farm labourers at nine shillings and at seven shillings a week; Scotch farm-labourers who, 'in districts the half of whose husbandry is that of cows, taste no milk, can procure no milk:' all these things are credible to us; several of them are known to us by the best evidence, by eye-sight. With all this it is consistent that the wages of 'skilled labour' as it is called, should in many cases be higher than they ever were: the giant Steamengine in a giant English Nation will here create violent demand for labour, and will there annihilate demand. But, alas, the great portion of labour is not skilled: the millions are and must be skilless, where strength alone is wanted; ploughers, delvers, borers; hewers of wood and drawers of water; menials of the Steamengine, only the *chief* menials and immediate *body-servants* of which require skill. English Commerce stretches its fibres over the whole earth; sensitive literally, nay quivering in convulsion, to the farthest influences of the earth. The huge demon of Mechanism smokes and thunders, panting at his great task, in all sections of English land; changing his *shape* like a very Proteus; and infallibly at every change of shape, *oversetting* whole multitudes of workmen, and as if with the waving of his shadow from afar, hurling them asunder, this way and that, in their crowded march and course of work or traffic; so that the wisest no longer knows his whereabout. With an Ireland pouring daily in on us, in these circumstances; deluging us down to its own waste confusion, outward and inward, it seems a cruel mockery to tell poor drudges that *their* condition is improving.

New Poor-Law! *Laissez-faire, laissez-passer!* The master of horses, when the summer labour is done, has to feed his horses through the winter. If he said to his horses: " Quadrupeds, I have no longer work for you; but work exists abundantly over the world: are you ignorant (or must I read you Political-Economy Lectures) that the Steamengine always in the long-run creates additional work? Railways are forming in one quarter of this earth, canals in another, much cartage is wanted; somewhere in Europe, Asia, Africa or America, doubt it not, ye will find cartage: go and seek cartage, and good go with you!" They, with protrusive upper lip, snort dubious; signifying that Europe, Asia, Africa and America lie somewhat out of their beat; that what cartage may be wanted there is not too well known to them. *They* can find no cartage. They gallop distracted along highways, all fenced in to the right and to the left: finally, under pains of hunger, they take to leaping fences; eating foreign property, and—we know the rest. Ah, it is not a joyful mirth, it is sadder than tears, the laugh Humanity is forced to, at *Laissez-faire* applied to poor peasants, in a world like our Europe of the year 1839!

So much can observation altogether unstatistic, looking only at a Drogheda or Dublin steamboat, ascertain for itself. Another thing, likewise ascertainable on this vast obscure matter, excites a superficial surprise, but only a superficial one: That it is the best-paid workmen who, by Strikes, Trades-unions, Chartism, and the like, complain the most. No doubt of it! The best-paid workmen are they alone that *can* so complain! How shall he, the handloom weaver, who in the day that is passing over him has to find food for the day, strike work? If he strike work, he starves within the week. He is past complaint!—The fact itself, however, is one which, if we consider it, leads us into still deeper regions of the malady. Wages, it would appear, are no index of well-being to the working man: without proper wages there can be no well-being; but with them also there may be none. Wages of working men differ greatly in different quarters of this country; according to the researches or the guess of Mr. Symmons, an intelligent humane inquirer, they vary in the ratio of not less than three to one. Cotton-spinners, as we learn, are generally well paid, while employed; their wages, one week with another, wives and children all working, amount to sums which, if well laid out, were fully adequate to comfortable living. And yet, alas, there seems little question that comfort or reasonable well-being is as much a stranger in these households as in any. At the cold hearth of the ever-toiling ever-hungering weaver, dwells at least some equability, fixation as if in perennial ice: hope never comes; but also irregular impatience is absent. Of outward things these others have or might have enough, but of all inward things there is the fatallest lack. Economy does not exist among them; their trade now in plethoric prosperity, anon extenuated into inanition and 'short-time,' is of the nature of gambling; they live by it like gamblers, now in luxurious superfluity, now in starvation. Black mutinous discontent devours them; simply the miserablest feeling that can inhabit the heart of man. English Commerce with its worldwide convulsive fluctuations, with its immeasurable Proteus Steam-demon, makes all paths uncertain for them, all life a bewilderment: sobriety, steadfastness, peaceable continuance, the first blessings of man, are not theirs.

It is in Glasgow among that class of operatives that 'Number 60,' in his dark room, pays down the price of blood. Be it with reason or with unreason, too surely they do in verity find the time all out of joint; this world for them no home, but a dingy prison-house, of reckless unthrift, rebellion, rancour, indignation against themselves and against all men. Is it a green flowery world, with azure everlasting sky stretched over it, the work and government of a God; or a murky-simmering Tophet, of copperas-fumes, cotton-fuz, gin-riot, wrath and toil, created by a Demon, governed by a Demon? The sum of their wretchedness merited and unmerited welters, huge, dark and baleful, like a Dantean Hell, visible there in the statistics of Gin: Gin justly named the most authentic incarnation of the Infernal Principle in our times, too indisputable an incarnation; Gin the black throat into which wretchedness of every sort, consummating itself by calling on delirium to help it, whirls down; abdication of the power to think or resolve, as too painful now, on the part of men whose lot of all others would require thought and resolution; liquid Madness sold at ten-pence the quartern, all the products of which are and must be, like its origin, mad, miserable, ruinous, and that only! If from this black unluminous unheeded *Inferno*, and Prisonhouse of souls in pain, there do flash up from time to time, some dismal wide-spread glare of Chartism or the like, notable to all, claiming remedy from all,—are we to regard it as more baleful than the quiet state, or rather as not so baleful? Ireland is in chronic atrophy these five centuries; the disease of nobler England, identified now with that of Ireland, becomes acute, has crises, and will be cured or kill.

CHAPTER V.

RIGHTS AND MIGHTS.

It is not what a man outwardly has or wants that constitutes the happiness or misery of him. Nakedness, hunger, distress of all kinds, death itself have been cheerfully suffered, when the heart was right. It is the feeling of *injustice* that is insupportable to all men. The brutallest black African cannot bear that he should be used unjustly. No man can bear it, or ought to bear it. A deeper law than any parchment-law whatsoever, a law written direct by the hand of God in the inmost being of man, incessantly protests against it. What is injustice? Another name for *dis*order, for unveracity, unreality; a thing which veracious created Nature, even because it is not Chaos and a waste-whirling baseless Phantasm, rejects and disowns. It is not the outward pain of injustice; that, were it even the flaying of the back with knotted scourges, the severing of the head with guillotines, is comparatively a small matter. The real smart is the soul's pain and stigma, the hurt inflicted on the moral self. The rudest clown must draw himself up into attitude of battle, and resistance to the death, if such be offered him. He cannot live under it; his own soul aloud, and all the universe with silent continual beckonings, says. It cannot be. He must revenge himself; *revancher* himself, make himself good again,—that so *meum* may be mine, *tuum* thine, and each party standing clear on his own basis, order be restored. There is something infinitely respectable in this, and we may say universally respected; it is the common stamp of manhood vindicating itself in all of us, the basis of whatever is worthy in all of us, and through superficial diversities, the same in all.

As *dis*order, insane by the nature of it, is the hatefullest of things to man, who lives by sanity and order, so injustice is the worst evil, some call it the only evil, in this world. All men submit to toil, to disappointment, to unhappiness; it is their lot here; but in all hearts, inextinguishable by sceptic logic, by sorrow, perversion or despair itself, there is a small still voice intimating that it is not the final lot; that wild, waste, incoherent as it looks, a God presides over it; that it is not an injustice but a justice. Force itself, the hopelessness of resistance, has doubtless a composing effect;— against inanimate *Simooms*, and much other infliction of the like sort, we have found it suffice to produce complete composure. Yet, one would say, a permanent Injustice even from an Infinite Power would prove unendurable by men. If men had lost belief in a God, their only resource against a blind No-God, of Necessity and Mechanism, that held them like a hideous World-Steamengine, like a hideous Phalaris' Bull, imprisoned in its own iron belly, would be, with or without hope,—*revolt*. They could, as Novalis says, by a 'simultaneous universal act of suicide,' *depart* out of the World-Steamengine; and end, if not in victory, yet in invincibility, and unsubduable protest that such World-Steamengine was a failure and a stupidity.

Conquest, indeed, is a fact often witnessed; conquest, which seems mere wrong and force, everywhere asserts itself as a right among men. Yet if we examine, we shall find that, in this world, no conquest could ever become permanent, which did not withal shew itself beneficial to the conquered as well as to conquerors. Mithridates King of Pontus, come now to extremity, 'appealed to the patriotism of his people;' but, says the history, 'he had squeezed them, and fleeced and plundered them, for long years;' his requisitions, flying irregular, devastative, like the whirlwind, were less supportable than Roman strictness and method, regular though never so rigorous: he therefore appealed to their patriotism in vain. The Romans conquered Mithridates. The Romans, having conquered the world, held it conquered, *because*they could best govern the world; the mass of men found it nowise pressing to revolt; their fancy might be afflicted more or less, but in their solid interests they were better off than before. So too in this England long ago, the old Saxon Nobles, disunited among themselves, and in power too nearly equal, could not have governed the country well; Harold being slain, their last chance of governing it, except in anarchy and civil war, was over: a new class of strong Norman Nobles, entering with a strong man, with a succession of strong men at the head of them, and not disunited, but united by many ties, by their very community of language and interest, had there been no other, *were* in a condition to govern it; and did govern it, we can believe, in some rather tolerable manner, or they would not have continued there. They acted, little conscious of such function on their part, as an immense volunteer Police Force, stationed everywhere, united, disciplined, feudally regimented, ready for action; strong Teutonic men; who on the whole proved effective men, and drilled this wild Teutonic people into unity and peaceable co-operation better than others could have done! How *can-do*, if we will well interpret it, unites itself with *shall-do* among mortals; how strength acts ever as the right-arm of justice; how might and right, so frightfully discrepant at first, are ever in the long-run one and the same,—is a cheering consideration, which always in the black tempestuous vortices of this world's history, will shine out on us, like an everlasting polar star.

Of conquest we may say that it never yet went by brute force and compulsion; conquest of that kind does not endure. Conquest, along with power of compulsion, an essential universally in human society, must bring benefit along with it, or men, of the ordinary strength of men, will fling it out. The strong man, what is he if we will consider? The wise man; the man with the gift of method, of faithfulness and valour, all of which are of the basis of wisdom; who has insight into what is what, into what will follow out of what, the eye to see and the hand to do; who is *fit* to administer, to direct, and guidingly command: he is the strong man. His muscles and bones are no stronger than ours; but his soul is stronger, his soul is wiser, clearer,—is better and nobler, for that is, has been, and ever will be the root of all clearness worthy of such a name. Beautiful it is, and a gleam from the same eternal pole-star visible amid the destinies of men, that all talent, all intellect is in the first place moral;—what a world were this otherwise! But it is the heart always that sees, before the head *can* see: let us know that; and know therefore that the Good alone is deathless and victorious, that Hope is sure and steadfast, in all phases of this 'Place of Hope.'—Shiftiness, quirk, attorney-cunning is a kind of thing that fancies itself, and is often fancied, to be talent; but it is luckily mistaken in that. Succeed truly it does, what is called succeeding; and even must in general succeed, if the dispensers of success be of due stupidity: men of due stupidity will needs say to it, "*Thou* art wisdom, rule thou!" Whereupon it rules. But Nature answers, "No, this ruling of thine is not according to *my* laws; thy wisdom was not wise enough! Dost thou take me too for a Quackery? For a Conventionality and Attorneyism? This chaff that thou sowest into my bosom, though it pass at the poll-booth and elsewhere for seed-corn, *I* will not grow wheat out of it, for it is chaff!"

But to return. Injustice, infidelity to truth and fact and Nature's order, being properly the one evil under the sun, and the feeling of injustice the one intolerable pain under the sun, our grand question as to the condition of these working men would be: Is it just? And first of all, What belief have they themselves formed about the justice of it? The words they promulgate are notable by way of answer; their actions are still more notable. Chartism with its pikes, Swing with his tinder-box, speak a most loud though inarticulate language. Glasgow Thuggery speaks aloud too, in a language we may well call infernal. What kind of * wild-justice' must it be in the hearts of these men that prompts them, with cold deliberation, in conclave assembled, to doom their brother workman, as the deserter of his order and his order's cause, to die as a traitor and deserter; and have him executed, since not by any public judge and hangman, then by a private one;—like your old Chivalry *Femgericht*, and Secret-Tribunal, suddenly in this strange guise become new; suddenly rising once more on the astonished eye, dressed now not in mail-shirts but in fustian jackets, meeting not in Westphalian forests but in the paved Gallowgate of Glasgow! Not loyal loving obedience to those placed over them, but a far other temper, must animate these men! It is frightful enough. Such temper must be wide-spread, virulent among the many, when even in its worst acme, it can take such a form in a few. But indeed decay of loyalty in all senses, disobedience, decay of religious faith, has long been noticeable and lamentable in this largest class, as in other smaller ones. Revolt, sullen revengeful humour of revolt against the upper classes, decreasing respect for what their temporal superiors command, decreasing faith for what their spiritual superiors teach, is more and more the universal spirit of the lower classes. Such spirit may be blamed, may be vindicated; but all men must recognise it as extant there, all may know that it is mournful, that unless altered it will be fatal. Of lower classes so related to upper, happy nations are not made! To whatever other griefs the lower classes labour under, this bitterest and sorest grief now superadds itself: the unendurable conviction that they are unfairly dealt with, that their lot in this world is not founded on right, not even on necessity and might, is neither what it should be, nor what it shall be.

Or why do we ask of Chartism, Glasgow Trades-unions, and such like? Has not broad Europe heard the question put, and answered, on the great scale; has not a FRENCH REVOLUTION been? Since the year 1789, there is now half-a-century complete; and a French Revolution not yet complete! Whosoever will look at that enormous Phenomenon may find many meanings in it, but this meaning as the ground of all: That it was a revolt of the oppressed lower classes against the oppressing or neglecting upper classes: not a French revolt only; no, a European one; full of stern monition to all countries of Europe. These Chartisms, Radicalisms, Reform Bill, Tithe Bill, and infinite other discrepancy, and acrid argument and jargon that there is yet to be, are *our* French Revolution: God grant that we, with our better methods, may be able to transact it by argument alone!

The French Revolution, now that we have sufficiently execrated its horrors and crimes, is found to have had withal a great meaning in it. As indeed, what great thing ever happened in this world, a world understood always to be made and governed by a Providence and Wisdom, not by an Unwisdom, without meaning somewhat? It was a tolerably audible voice of proclamation, and universal *oyez!* to all people, this of three-and-twenty years' close fighting, sieging, conflagrating, with a million or two of men shot dead: the world ought to know by this time that it was verily meant in earnest, that same Phenomenon, and had its own reasons for appearing there! Which accordingly the world begins now to do. The French Revolution is seen, or begins everywhere to be seen, 'as the crowning phenomenon of our Modern Time;' 'the inevitable stern end of much; the fearful, but also wonderful, indispensable and sternly beneficent beginning of much.' He who would understand the struggling convulsive unrest of European society, in any and every country, at this day, may read it in broad glaring lines there, in that the most convulsive phenomenon of the last thousand years. Europe lay pining, obstructed, moribund; quack-ridden, hag-ridden,—is there a hag, or spectre of the Pit, so baleful, hideous as your accredited quack, were he never so close-shaven, mild-spoken, plausible to himself and others? Quack-ridden: in that one word lies all misery whatsoever. Speciosity in all departments usurps the place of reality, thrusts reality away; instead of performance, there is appearance of performance. The quack is a Falsehood Incarnate; and speaks, and makes and does mere falsehoods, which Nature with her veracity has to disown. As chief priest, as chief governor, he stands there, intrusted with much. The husbandman of 'Time's Seedfield;' he is the world's hired sower, hired and solemnly appointed to sow the kind true earth with wheat this year, that next year all men may have bread. He, miserable mortal, deceiving and self-deceiving, sows it, as we said, not with corn but with chaff; the world nothing doubting, harrows it in, pays him his wages, dismisses him with blessing, and—next year there has no corn sprung. Nature has disowned the chaff, declined growing chaff, and behold now there is no bread! It becomes necessary, in such case, to do several things; not soft things some of them, but hard.

Nay we will add that the very circumstance of quacks in unusual quantity getting domination, indicates that the heart of the world is *already* wrong. The impostor is false; but neither are his dupes altogether true: is not his first grand dupe the falsest of all,—himself namely? Sincere men, of never so limited intellect, have an instinct for discriminating sincerity. The cunningest Mephistopheles cannot deceive a simple Margaret of honest heart; 'it stands written on his brow.' Masses of people capable of being led away by quacks are themselves of partially untrue spirit. Alas, in such times it grows to be the universal belief, sole accredited knowingness, and the contrary of it accounted puerile enthusiasm, this sorrowfullest *disbelief* that there is properly speaking any truth in the world; that the world was, has been, or ever can be guided, except by simulation, dissimulation, and the sufficiently dexterous practice of pretence. The faith of men is dead: in what has guineas in its pocket, beefeaters riding behind it, and cannons trundling before it, they can believe; in what has none of these things they cannot believe. Sense for the true and false is lost; there is properly no longer any true or false. It is the heyday of Imposture; of Semblance recognising itself, and getting itself recognised, for Substance. Gaping multitudes listen; unlistening multitudes see not but that it is all right, and in the order of Nature. Earnest men, one of a million, shut their lips; suppressing thoughts, which there are no words to utter. To them it is too visible that spiritual life has departed; that material life, in whatsoever figure of it, cannot long remain behind. To them it seems as if our Europe of the Eighteenth Century, long hag-ridden, vexed with foul enchanters, to the length now of gorgeous Domdaniel *Parcs-aux-cerfs* and 'Peasants living on meal-husks and boiled grass,' had verily sunk down to die and dissolve; and were now, with its French Philosophisms, Hume Scepticisms, Diderot Atheisms, maundering in the final deliration; writhing, with its Seven-years Silesian robber-wars, in the final agony. Glory to God, our Europe was not to die but to live! Our Europe rose like a frenzied giant; shook all that poisonous magician trumpery to right and left, trampling it storm-fully under foot; and declared aloud that there was strength in him, not for life only, but for new and infinitely wider life. Antæus-like the giant had struck his foot once more upon Reality and the Earth; there only, if in this universe at all, lay strength and healing for him. Heaven knows, it was not a gentle process; no wonder that it was a fearful process, this same 'Phoenix fire-consummation!' But the alternative was it or death; the merciful Heavens, merciful in their severity, sent us it rather.

And so the 'rights of man' were to be written down on paper; and experimentally wrought upon towards elaboration, in huge battle and wrestle, element conflicting with element, from side to side of this earth, for three-and-twenty years. Rights of man, wrongs of man? It is a question which has swallowed whole nations and generations; a question—on which we will not enter here. Far be it from us! Logic has small business with this question at present; logic has no plummet that will sound it at any time. But indeed the rights of man, as has been not unaptly remarked, are little worth ascertaining in comparison to the *mights* of man,—to what portion of his rights he has any chance of being able to make good? The accurate final rights of man lie in the far deeps of the Ideal, where 'the Ideal weds itself to the Possible,' as the Philosophers say. The ascertainable temporary rights of man vary not a little, according to place and time. They are known to depend much on what a man's convictions of them are. The Highland wife, with her husband at the foot of the gallows, patted him on the shoulder (if there be historical truth in Joseph Miller), and said amid her tears: "Go up, Donald, my man; the Laird bids ye." To her it seemed the rights of lairds were great, the rights of men small; and she acquiesced. Deputy Lapoule, in the *Salle des Menus* at Versailles, on the 4th of August, 1789, demanded (he did actually demand,' and by unanimous vote obtain) that the 'obsolete law' authorizing a Seigneur, on his return from the chase or other needful fatigue, to slaughter not above two of his vassals, and refresh his feet in their warm blood and bowels, should be 'abrogated.' From such obsolete law, or mad tradition and phantasm of an obsolete law, down to any corn-law, game-law, rotten-borough law, or other law or practice clamoured of in this time of ours, the distance travelled over is great!—What are the rights of men? All men are justified in demanding and searching for their rights; moreover, justified or not, they will do it: by Chartisms, Radicalisms, French Revolutions, or whatsoever methods they have. Rights surely are right: on the other hand, this other saying is most true, 'Use every man according to his *rights* and who shall escape whipping?' These two things, we say, are both true; and both are essential to make up the whole truth. All good men know always and feel, each for himself, that the one is not less true than the other; and act accordingly. The contradiction is of the surface only; as in opposite sides of the same fact: universal in this *dualism* of a life we have. Between these two extremes. Society and all human things must fluctuatingly adjust themselves the best they can.

And yet that there is verily a 'rights of man' let no mortal doubt. An ideal of right does dwell in all men, in all arrangements, pactions and procedures of men: it is to this ideal of right, more and more developing itself as it is more and more approximated to, that human Society for ever tends and struggles. We say also that any given thing either *is* unjust or else just; however obscure the arguings and strugglings on it be, the thing in itself there as it lies, infallibly enough, *is* the one or the other. To which let us add only this, the first, last article of faith, the alpha and omega of all faith among men. That nothing which is unjust can hope to continue in this world. A faith true in all times, more or less forgotten in most, but altogether frightfully brought to remembrance again in ours! Lyons fusilladings, Nantes noyadings, reigns of terror, and such other universal battle-thunder and explosion; these, if we will understand them, were but a new irrefragable preaching abroad of that. It would appear that Speciosities which are not Realities cannot any longer inhabit this world. It would appear that the unjust thing has no friend in the Heaven, and a majority against it on the Earth; nay that *it* has at bottom all men for its enemies; that it may take shelter in this fallacy and then in that, but will be hunted from fallacy to fallacy till it find no fallacy to shelter in any more, but must march and go elsewhither;—that, in a word, it ought to prepare incessantly for decent departure, before *in*decent departure, ignominious drumming out, nay savage smiting out and burning out, overtake it! Alas, was that such new tidings? Is it not from of old indubitable, that Untruth, Injustice which is but acted untruth, has no power to continue in this true universe of ours? The tidings was world-old, or older, as old as the Fall of Lucifer: and yet in that epoch unhappily it was new tidings, unexpected, incredible; and there had to be such earthquakes and shakings of the nations before it could be listened to, and laid to heart even slightly! Let us lay it to heart, let us know it well, that new shakings be not needed. Known and laid to heart it must everywhere be, before peace can pretend to come. This seems to us the secret of our convulsed era; this which is so easily written, which is and has been and will be so hard to bring to pass. All true men, high and low, each in his sphere, are consciously or unconsciously bringing it to pass; all false and half-true men are fruitlessly spending themselves to hinder it from coming to pass.

CHAPTER VI.
LAISSEZ-FAIRE.

FROM all which enormous events, with truths old and new embodied in them, what innumerable practical inferences are to be drawn! Events are written lessons, glaring in huge hieroglyphic picture-writing, that all may read and know them: the terror and horror they inspire is but the note of preparation for the truth they are to teach; a mere waste of terror if that be not learned. Inferences enough; most didactic, practically applicable in all departments of English things! One inference, but one inclusive of all, shall content us here; this namely: That *Laissez-faire* has as good as done its part in a great many provinces; that in the province of the Working Classes, *Laissez-faire* having passed its New Poor-Law, has reached the suicidal point, and now, as *felo-de-se*, lies dying there, in torchlight meetings and such like; that, in brief, a government of the under classes by the upper on a principle of *Let alone* is no longer possible in England in these days. This is the one inference inclusive of all. For there can be no acting or doing of any kind, till it be recognised that there is a thing to be done; the thing once recognised, doing in a thousand shapes becomes possible. The Working Classes cannot any longer go on without government; without being *actually* guided and governed; England cannot subsist in peace till, by some means or other, some guidance and government for them is found.

For, alas, on us too the rude truth has come home. Wrappages and speciosities all worn off, the haggard naked fact speaks to us: Are these millions taught? Are these millions guided? We have a Church, the venerable embodiment of an idea which may well call itself divine; which our fathers for long ages, feeling it to be divine, have been embodying as we see: it is a Church well furnished with equipments and appurtenances; educated in universities; rich in money; set on high places that it may be conspicuous to all, honoured of all. We have an Aristocracy of landed wealth and commercial wealth, in whose hands lies the law-making and the law-administering; an Aristocracy rich, powerful, long secure in its place; an Aristocracy with more faculty put free into its hands than was ever before, in any country or time, put into the hands of any class of men. This Church answers: Yes, the people are taught. This Aristocracy, astonishment in every feature, answers: Yes, surely the people are guided! Do we not pass what Acts of Parliament are needful; as many as thirty-nine for the shooting of the partridges alone? Are there not treadmills, gibbets; even hospitals, poor-rates, New Poor-Law? So answers Church; so answers Aristocracy, astonishment in every feature.—Fact, in the meanwhile, takes his lucifer-box, sets fire to wheat-stacks; sheds an all-too dismal light on several things. Fact searches for his third-rate potatoe, not in the meekest humour, six-and-thirty weeks each year; and does not find it Fact passionately joins Messiah Thom of Canterbury, and has himself shot for a new fifth-monarchy brought in by Bedlam. Fact holds his fustian-jacket *Femgericht* in Glasgow City. Fact carts his Petition over London streets, begging that you would simply have the goodness to grant him universal suffrage, and 'the five points' by way of remedy. These are not symptoms of teaching and guiding.

Nay, at bottom, is it not a singular thing this of *Laissez-faire* from the first origin of it? As good as an *abdication* on the part of governors; an admission that they are henceforth incompetent to govern, that they are not there to govern at all, but to do—one knows not what! The universal demand of *Laissez-faire* by a people from its governors or upper classes, is a soft-sounding demand; but it is only one step removed from the fatallest. '*Laissez-faire*,' exclaims a sardonic German writer, 'What is this universal cry for *Laissez-faire?* Does it mean that human affairs require no guidance; that wisdom and forethought cannot guide them better than folly and accident? Alas, does it not mean: *Such* guidance is worse than none! Leave us alone of *your* guidance; eat your wages, and sleep!" 'And now if guidance have grown indispensable, and the sleep continue, what becomes of the sleep and its wages?—In those entirely surprising circumstances to which the Eighteenth Century had brought us, in the time of Adam Smith, *Laissez-faire* was a reasonable cry;—as indeed, in all circumstances, for a wise governor there will be meaning in the principle of it. To wise governors you will cry: "See what you will, and will not, let alone." To unwise governors, to hungry Greeks throttling down hungry Greeks on the floor of a St. Stephens, you will cry: "Let *all* things alone; for Heaven's sake, meddle ye with nothing!" How *Laissez-faire* may adjust itself in other provinces we say not: but we do venture to say, and ask whether events everywhere, in world-history and parish-history, in all manner of dialects are not saying it. That in regard to the lower orders of society, and their governance and guidance, the principle of *Laissez-faire* has terminated, and is no longer applicable at all, in this Europe of ours, still less in this England of ours. Not misgovernment, nor yet no-government; only government will now serve. What is the meaning of the 'five points,' if we will understand them? What are all popular commotions and maddest bellowings, from Peterloo to the Place-de-Grève itself? Bellowings, *in*articulate cries as of a dumb creature in rage and pain; to the ear of wisdom they are inarticulate prayers: "Guide me, govern me! I am mad, and miserable, and cannot guide myself!" Surely of all 'rights of man,' this right of the ignorant man to be guided by the wiser, to be, gently or forcibly, held in the true course by him, is the indisputablest. Nature herself ordains it from the first; Society struggles towards perfection by enforcing and accomplishing it more and more. If Freedom have any meaning, it means enjoyment of this right, wherein all other rights are enjoyed. It is a sacred right and duty, on both sides; and the summary of all social duties whatsoever between the two. Why does the one toil with his hands, if the other be not to toil, still more unweariedly, with heart and head? The brawny craftsman finds it no child's play to mould his unpliant rugged masses; neither is guidance of men a dilettantism: what it becomes when treated as a dilettantism, we may see! The wild horse bounds homeless through the wilderness, is not led to stall and manger; but neither does he toil for you, but for himself only.

Democracy, we are well aware, what is called 'self-government' of the multitude by the multitude, is in words the thing everywhere passionately clamoured for at present. Democracy makes rapid progress in these latter times, and ever more rapid, in a perilous accelerative ratio; towards democracy, and that only, the progress of things is everywhere tending as to the final goal and winning-post. So think, so clamour the multitudes everywhere. And yet all men may see, whose sight is good for much, that in democracy can lie no finality; that with the completest winning of democracy there is nothing yet won,—except emptiness, and the free chance to win! Democracy is, by the nature of it, a self-cancelling business; and gives in the long-run a net-result of *zero*. Where no government is wanted, save that of the parish-constable, as in America with its boundless soil, every man being able to find work and recompense for himself, democracy may subsist; not elsewhere, except briefly, as a swift transition towards something other and farther. Democracy never yet, that we heard of, was able to accomplish much work, beyond that same cancelling of itself. Rome and Athens are themes for the schools; unexceptionable for that purpose. In Rome and Athens, as elsewhere, if we look practically, we shall find that it was not by loud voting and debating of many, but by wise insight and ordering of a few that the work was done. So is it ever, so will it ever be. The French Convention was a Parliament elected 'by the five point,' with ballot-boxes, universal suffrages, and what not, as perfectly as Parliament can hope to be in this world; and had indeed a pretty spell of work to do, and did it. The French Convention had to cease from being a free Parliament, and become more arbitrary than any Sultan Bajazet before it could so much as subsist. It had to purge out its argumentative Girondins, elect its Supreme Committee of *Salut*, guillotine into silence and extinction all that gainsayed it, and rule and work literally by the sternest despotism ever seen in Europe, before it could rule at all. Napoleon was not president of a republic; Cromwell tried hard to rule in that way, but found that he could not. These, 'the armed soldiers of democracy,' had to chain democracy under their feet, and become despots over it, before they could work out the earnest obscure purpose of democracy itself! Democracy, take it where you will in our Europe, is found but as a regulated method of rebellion and abrogation; it abrogates the old arrangement of things; and leaves, as we say, *zero* and vacuity for the institution of a new arrangement. It is the consummation of No-government and *Laissez-faire*. It may be natural for our Europe at present; but cannot be the ultimatum of it. Not towards the impossibility, 'self-government' of a multitude by a multitude; but towards some possibility, government by the wisest, does bewildered Europe struggle. The blessedest possibility: not misgovernment, not *Laissez-faire*, but veritable government! Cannot one discern too, across all democratic turbulence, clattering of ballot-boxes and infinite sorrowful jangle, needful or not, that this at bottom is the wish and prayer of all human hearts, everywhere and at all times: "Give me a leader; a true leader, not a false sham-leader; a true leader, that he may guide me on the true way, that I may be loyal to him, that I may swear fealty to him and follow him, and feel that it is well with me!" The relation of the taught to their teacher, of the loyal subject to his guiding king, is, under one shape or another, the vital element of human Society; indispensable to it, perennial in it; without which, as a body reft of its soul, it falls down into death, and with horrid noisome dissolution passes away and disappears.

But verily in these times, with their new stern Evangel, that Speciosities which are not Realities can no longer be, all Aristocracies, Priesthoods, Persons in Authority, are called upon to consider. What is an Aristocracy? A corporation of the Best, of the Bravest. To this joyfully, with heart-loyalty, do men pay the half of their substance, to equip and decorate their Best, to lodge them in palaces, set them high over all. For it is of the nature of men, in every time, to honour and love their Best; to know no limits in honouring them. Whatsoever Aristocracy *is* still a corporation of the Best, is safe from all peril, and the land it rules is a safe and blessed land. Whatsoever Aristocracy does not even attempt to be that, but only to wear the clothes of that, is not safe; neither is the land it rules in safe! For this now is our sad lot, that we must find a *real*Aristocracy, that an apparent Aristocracy, how plausible soever, has become inadequate for us. One way or other, the world will absolutely need to be governed; if not by this class of men, then by that. One can predict, without gift of prophecy, that the era of routine is nearly ended. Wisdom and faculty alone, faithful, valiant, ever-zealous, not pleasant but painful, continual effort, will suffice. Cost what it may, by one means or another, the toiling multitudes of this perplexed, over-crowded Europe, must and will find governors. '*Laissez-faire*, Leave them to do?' The thing they will *do*, if so left, is too frightful to think of! It has been done once, in sight of the whole earth, in these generations: can it need to be done a second time?

For a Priesthood, in like manner, whatsoever its titles, possessions, professions, there is but one question: Does it teach and spiritually guide this people, yea or no? If yea, then is all well. But if no, then let it strive earnestly to alter, for as yet there is nothing well! Nothing, we say: and indeed is not this that we call spiritual guidance properly the soul of the whole, the life and eyesight of the whole? The world asks of its Church in these times, more passionately than of any other Institution any question, "Canst thou teach us or not?"—A Priesthood in France, when the world asked, "What canst thou do for us?" answered only, aloud and ever louder, "Are we not of God? Invested with all power?"—till at length France cut short this controversy too, in what frightful way we know. To all men who believed in the Church, to all men who believed in God and the soul of man, there was no issue of the French Revolution half so sorrowful as that. France cast out its benighted blind Priesthood into destruction; yet with what a loss to France also! A solution of continuity, what we may well call such; and this where continuity is so momentous: the New, whatever it may be, cannot now *grow* out of the Old, but is severed sheer asunder from the Old,—how much lies wasted in that gap! That one whole generation of thinkers should be without a religion to believe, or even to contradict; that Christianity, in thinking France, should as it were fade away so long into a remote extraneous tradition, was one of the saddest facts connected with the future of that country. Look at such Political and Moral Philosophies, St.-Simonisms, Robert-Macairisms, and the 'Literature of Desperation'! Kingship was perhaps but a cheap waste, compared with this of the Priestship; under which France still, all but unconsciously, labours; and may long labour, remediless the while. Let others consider it, and take warning by it! France is a pregnant example in all ways. Aristocracies that do not govern. Priesthoods that do not teach; the misery of that, and the misery of altering that,—are written in Belshazzar fire-letters on the history of France.

Or does the British reader, safe in the assurance that 'England is not France,' call all this unpleasant doctrine of ours ideology, perfectibility, and a vacant dream? Does the British reader, resting on the faith that what has been these two generations was from the beginning, and will be to the end, assert to himself that things are already as they can be, as they must be; that on the whole, no Upper Classes did ever 'govern' the Lower, in this sense of governing? Believe it not, O British reader! Man is man everywhere; dislikes to have 'sensible species' and 'ghosts of defunct bodies' foisted on him, in England even as in France. How much the Upper Classes did actually, in any the most perfect Feudal time, return to the Under by way of recompense, in government, guidance, protection, we will not undertake to specify here. In Charity-Balls, Soup-Kitchens, in Quarter-

Sessions, Prison-Discipline and Treadmills, we can well believe the old Feudal Aristocracy not to have surpassed the new. Yet we do say that the old Aristocracy were the governors of the Lower Classes, the guides of the Lower Classes; and even, at bottom, that they existed as an Aristocracy because they were found adequate for that. Not by Charity-Balls and Soup-Kitchens; not so; far otherwise! But it was their happiness that, in struggling for their own objects, they had to govern the Lower Classes, even in this sense of governing. For, in one word, *Cash Payment* had not then grown to be the universal sole nexus of man to man; it was something other than money that the high then expected from the low, and could not live without getting from the low. Not as buyer and seller alone, of land or what else it might be, but in many senses still as soldier and captain, as clansman and head, as loyal subject and guiding king, was the low related to the high. With the supreme triumph of Cash, a changed time has entered; there must a changed Aristocracy enter. We invite the British reader to meditate earnestly on these things.

Another thing, which the British reader often reads and hears in this time, is worth his meditating for a moment: That Society 'exists for the protection of property.' To which it is added, that the poor man also has property, namely, his 'labour,' and the fifteen-pence or three-and-sixpence a-day he can get for that. True enough, O friends, 'for protecting *property*;' most true: and indeed if you will once sufficiently enforce that Eighth Commandment, the whole 'rights of man' are well cared for; I know no better definition of the rights of man. *Thou shalt not steal, thou shalt not be stolen from:* what a Society were that; Plato's Republic, More's Utopia mere emblems of it! Give every man what is his, the accurate price of what he has done and been, no man shall any more complain, neither shall the earth suffer any more. For the protection of property, in very truth, and for that alone!—And now what is thy property? That parchment title-deed, that purse thou buttonest in thy breeches-pocket? Is that thy valuable property? Unhappy brother, most poor insolvent brother, I without parchment at all, with purse oftenest in the flaccid state, imponderous, which will not fling against the wind, have quite other property than that! I have the miraculous breath of Life in me, breathed into my nostrils Almighty God. I have affections, thoughts, a god-given *capability* to be and do; rights, therefore,—

the right for instance to thy love if I love thee, to thy guidance if I obey thee: the strangest rights, whereof in church-pulpits one still hears something, though almost unintelligible now; rights, stretching high into Immensity, far into Eternity! Fifteen-pence a-day; three-and-sixpence a-day; eight hundred pounds and odd a-day, dost thou call that my property? I value that little; little all I could purchase with that. For truly, as is said, what matters it? In torn boots, in soft-hung carriages-and-four, a man gets always to his journey's end. Socrates walked barefoot, or in wooden shoes, and yet arrived happily. They never asked him. *What* shoes or conveyance? never, What wages hadst thou? but simply. What work didst thou?—Property, O brother? 'Of my very body I have but a life-rent.' As for this flaccid purse of mine, 'tis something, nothing; has been the slave of pickpockets, cutthroats, Jew-brokers, gold-dust-robbers; 'twas his, 'tis mine;—'tis thine, if thou care much to steal it. But my soul, breathed into me by God, my *Me* and what capability is there; that is mine, and I will resist the stealing of it. I call that mine and not thine; I will keep that, and do what work I can with it: God has given it me, the Devil shall not take it away! Alas, my friends, Society exists and has existed for a great many purposes, not so easy to specify!

Society, it is understood, does not in any age, prevent a man from being what he *can be*. A sooty African can become a Toussaint L'ouverture, a murderous Three-fingered Jack, let the yellow West Indies say to it what they will. A Scottish poet 'proud of his name and country,' *can* apply fervently to 'Gentlemen of the Caledonian Hunt,' and become a ganger of beer-barrels, and tragical immortal broken-hearted Singer; the stifled echo of his melody audible through long centuries, one other note in 'that sacred *Miserere*' that rises up to Heaven, out of all times and lands. What I *can be* thou decidedly wilt not hinder me from being. Nay even for being what I *could be*, I have the strangest claims on thee, —not convenient to adjust at present! Protection of breeches-pocket property? O reader, to what shifts is poor Society reduced, struggling to give still some account of herself, in epochs when Cash Payment has become the sole nexus of man to men! On the whole, we will advise Society not to talk at all about what she exists for; but rather with her whole industry to exist, to try how she can keep existing! That is her best plan. She may depend upon it, if she ever, by cruel chance, did come to exist only for protection of breeches-pocket property, she would lose very soon the gift of protecting even that, and find her career in our lower world on the point of terminating!—

For the rest, that in the most perfect Feudal Ages, the Ideal of Aristocracy nowhere lived in vacant serene purity as an Ideal, but always as a poor imperfect Actual, little heeding or not knowing at all that an Ideal lay in it,—this too we will cheerfully admit. Imperfection, it is known, cleaves to human things; far is the Ideal departed from, in most times; very far! And yet so long as an Ideal (any soul of Truth) does, in never so confused a manner, exist and work within the Actual, it is a tolerable business. Not so, when the Ideal has entirely departed, and the Actual owns to itself that it has no Idea, no soul of Truth any longer: at that degree of imperfection human things cannot continue living; they are obliged to alter or expire, when they attain to that. Blotches and diseases exist on the skin and deeper, the heart continuing whole; but it is another matter when the heart itself becomes diseased; when there is no heart, but a monstrous gangrene pretending to exist there as heart!

On the whole, O reader, thou wilt find everywhere that things which have had an existence among men have first of all had to have a truth and worth in them, and were not semblances but realities. Nothing not a reality ever yet got men to pay bed and board to it for long. Look at Mahometanism itself! Dalai-Lamaism, even Dalai-Lamaism, one rejoices to discover, may be worth its victuals in this world; not a quackery but a sincerity; not a nothing but a something! The mistake of those who believe that fraud, force, injustice, whatsoever untrue thing, howsoever cloaked and decorated, was ever or can ever be the principle of man's relations to man, is great, and the greatest. It is the error of the infidel; in whom the truth as yet is *not*. It is an error pregnant with mere errors and miseries; an error fatal, lamentable, to be abandoned by all men.

CHAPTER VII.

NOT LAISSEZ-FAIRE

How an Aristocracy, in these present times and circumstances, could, if never so well disposed, set about governing the Under Class? What they should do; endeavour or attempt to do? That is even the question of questions:—the question which *they* have to solve; which it is our utmost function at present to tell them, lies there for solving, and must and will be solved.

Insoluble we cannot fancy it. One select class Society has furnished with wealth, intelligence, leisure, means outward and inward for governing; another huge class, furnished by Society with none of those things, declares that it must be governed: Negative stands fronting Positive; if Negative and Positive *cannot*unite,—it will be worse for both! Let the faculty and earnest constant effort of England combine round this matter; let it once be recognised as a vital matter. Innumerable things our Upper Classes and Lawgivers might 'do;' but the preliminary of all things, we must repeat, is to know that a thing must needs be done. We lead them here to the shore of a boundless continent; ask them. Whether they do not with their own eyes see it, see strange symptoms of it, lying huge, dark, unexplored, inevitable; full of hope, but also full of difficulty, savagery, almost of despair? Let them enter; they must enter; Time and Necessity have brought them hither; where they are is no continuing! Let them enter; the first step once taken, the next will have become clearer, all future steps will become possible. It is a great problem for all of us; but for themselves, we may say, more than for any. On them chiefly, as the expected solvers of it, will the failure of a solution first fall. One way or other there must and will be a solution.

True, these matters lie far, very far indeed, from the 'usual habits of Parliament,' in late times; from the routine course of any Legislative or Administrative body of men that exists among us. Too true! And that is even the thing we complain of: had the mischief been looked into as it gradually rose, it would not have attained this magnitude. That self-cancelling Donothingism and *Laissez-faire* should have got so ingrained into our Practice, is the source of all these miseries. It is too true that Parliament, for the matter of near a century now, has been able to undertake the adjustment of almost one thing alone, of itself and its own interests; leaving other interests to rub along very much as they could and would. True, this was the practice of the whole Eighteenth Century; and struggles still to prolong itself into the Nineteenth,—which however is no longer the time for it! Those Eighteenth-century Parliaments, one may hope, will become a curious object one day. Are not these same '*Mémoires*' of Horace Walpole, to an unparliamentary eye, already a curious object? One of the clearest-sighted men of the Eighteenth Century writes down his Parliamentary observation of it there; a determined despiser and merciless dissector of cant; a liberalwithal, one who will go all lengths for the 'glorious revolution,' and resist Tory principles to the death: he writes, with an indignant elegiac feeling, how Mr. This, who had voted so and then voted so, and was the son of this and the brother of that, and had such claims to the fat appointment, was nevertheless scandalously postponed to Mr. That;—whereupon are not the affairs of this nation in a bad way? How hungry Greek meets hungry Greek on the floor of St. Stephens, and wrestles him and throttles him till he has to cry, Hold! the office is thine!—of this does Horace write.—One must say, the destinies of nations do not always rest entirely on Parliament. One must say, it is a wonderful Affair that science of 'government,' as practised in the Eighteenth Century of the Christian era, and still struggling to practise itself. One must say, it was a lucky century that could get it so practised: a century which had inherited richly from its predecessors; and also which did, not unnaturally, bequeath to its successors a French Revolution, general overturn, and reign of terror;—intimating, in most audible thunder, conflagration, guillotinement, cannonading and universal war and earthquake, that such century with its practices had *ended*.

Ended;—for decidedly that course of procedure will no longer serve. Parliament will absolutely, with whatever effort, have to lift itself out of those deep ruts of donothing routine; and learn to say, on all sides, something more edifying than *Laissez-faire*. If Parliament cannot learn it, what is to become of Parliament? The toiling millions of England ask of their English Parliament foremost of all, Canst thou govern us or not? Parliament with its privileges is strong; but Necessity and the Laws of Nature are stronger than it. If Parliament cannot do this thing, Parliament we prophesy will do some other thing and things which, in the strangest and not the happiest way, will forward its being done,—not much to the advantage of Parliament probably! Done, one way or other, the thing must be. In these complicated times, with Cash Payment as the sole nexus between man and man, the Toiling Classes of mankind declare, in their confused but most emphatic way, to the Untoiling, that they will be governed; that they must,—under penalty of Chartisms, Thuggeries, Rick-burnings, and even blacker things than those. Vain also is it to think that the misery of one class, of the great universal under class, can be isolated, and kept apart and peculiar, down in that class. By infallible contagion, evident enough to reflection, evident even to Political Economy that will reflect, the misery of the lowest spreads upwards and upwards till it reaches the very highest; till all has grown miserable, palpably false and wrong; and poor drudges hungering 'on meal-husks and boiled grass' do, by circuitous but sure methods, bring kings' heads to the block!

Cash Payment the sole nexus; and there are so many things which cash will not pay! Cash is a great miracle; yet it has not all power in Heaven, nor even on Earth. 'Supply and demand' we will honour also; and yet how many 'demands' are there, entirely indispensable, which have to go elsewhere than to the shops, and produce quite other than cash, before they can get their supply? On the whole, what astonishingpayments does cash make in this world! Of your Samuel Johnson furnished with 'fourpence halfpenny a-day,' and solid lodging at nights on the paved streets, as his payment, we do not speak;—not in the way of complaint: it is a world-old business for the like of him, that same arrangement or a worse; perhaps the man, for his own uses, had need even of that and of no better. Nay is not Society, busy with its Talfourd Copyright Bill and the like, struggling to do something effectual for that man;—enacting with all industry that his own creation be accounted his own manufacture, and continue unstolen, on his own market-stand, for so long as sixty years? Perhaps Society is right there; for discrepancies on that side too may become excessive. All men are not patient docile Johnsons; some of them are half-mad inflammable Rousseaus. Such, in peculiar times, you may drive too far. Society in France, for example, was not destitute of cash: Society contrived to pay Philippe d'Orleans not yet Egalité three hundred thousand a-year and odd, for driving cabriolets through the streets of Paris and other work done: but in cash, encouragement, arrangement, recompense or recognition of any kind, it had nothing to give this same half-mad Rousseau for his work done; whose brain in consequence, *too* 'much enforced' for a weak brain, uttered hasty sparks, *Contrat Social* and the like, which proved not so quenchable again! In regard to that species of men too, who knows whether *Laissez-faire* itself (which is Sergeant Talfourd's Copyright Bill continued to eternity instead of sixty years) will not turn out insufficient, and have to cease, one day?—

Alas, in regard to so very many things. *Laissez-faire* ought partly to endeavour to cease! But in regard to poor Sanspotatoe peasants, Trades-Union craftsmen. Chartist cotton-spinners, the time has come when it must either cease or a worse thing straightway begin,—a thing of tinder-boxes, vitriol-bottles, second-hand pistols, a visibly insupportable thing in the eyes of all.

CHAPTER VIII.
NEW ERAS.

FOR in very truth it is a 'new Era;' a new Practice has become indispensable in it. One has heard so often of new eras, new and newest eras, that the word has grown rather empty of late. Yet new eras do come; there is no fact surer than that they have come more than once. And always with a change of era, with a change of intrinsic conditions, there had to be a change of practice and outward relations brought about,—if not peaceably, then by violence; for brought about it had to be, there could no rest come till then. How many eras and epochs, not noted at the moment; —which indeed is the blessedest condition of epochs, that they come quietly, making no proclamation of themselves, and are only visible long after: a Cromwell Rebellion, a French Revolution, 'striking on the Horologe of Time,' to tell all mortals what o'clock it has become, are too expensive, if one could help it!—

In a strange rhapsodic 'History of the Teuton Kindred (*Geschichte der Teutschen Sippschaft*),' not yet translated into our language, we have found a Chapter on the Eras of England, which, were there room for it, would be instructive in this place. We shall crave leave to excerpt some pages; partly as a relief from the too near vexations of our own rather sorrowful Era; partly as calculated to throw, more or less obliquely, some degree of light on the meanings of that. The Author is anonymous: but we have heard him called the Herr Professor Sauerteig, and indeed think we know him under that name:

'Who shall say what work and works this England has yet to do? For what purpose this land of Britain was created, set like a jewel in the encircling blue of Ocean; and this Tribe of Saxons, fashioned in the depths of Time, "on the shores of the Black Sea" or elsewhere, "out of Harzgebirge rock" or whatever other material, was sent travelling hitherward? No man can say: it was for a work, and for works, incapable of announcement in words. Thou seest them there; part of them stand done, and visible to the eye; even these thou canst not *name*: how much less the others still matter of prophecy only!—They live and labour there, these twenty million Saxon men; they have been born into this mystery of life out of the darkness of East Time:—how changed now since the first Father and first Mother of them set forth, quitting the Tribe of *Theuth*, with passionate farewell, under questionable auspices; on scanty bullock-cart, if they had even bullocks and a cart; with axe and hunting-spear, to subdue a portion of our common Planet! This Nation now has cities and seedfields, has spring-vans, dray-waggons, Long-acre carriages, nay railway trains; has coined-money, exchange-bills, laws, books, war-fleets, spinning-jennies, warehouses and West-India Docks: see what it has built and done, what it can and will yet build and do! These umbrageous pleasure-woods, green meadows, shaven stubble-fields, smooth-sweeping roads; these high-domed cities, and what they hold and bear; this mild Good-morrow which the stranger bids thee, equitable, nay forbearant if need were, judicially calm and law-observing towards thee a stranger, what work has it not cost? How many brawny arms, generation after generation, sank down wearied; how many noble hearts, toiling while life lasted, and wise heads that wore themselves dim with scanning and discerning, before this waste *Whitecliff*, Albion so-called, with its other Cassiterides *Tin Islands*, became a BRITISH EMPIRE! The stream of World-History has altered its complexion; Romans are dead out, English are come in. The red broad mark of Romanhood, stamped ineffaceably on that Chart of Time, has disappeared from the present, and belongs only to the past. England plays its part; England too has a mark to leave, and we will hope none of the least significant. Of a truth, whosoever had, with the bodily eye, seen Hengst and Horsa mooring on the mud-beach of Thanet, on that spring morning of the Year 449; and then, with the spiritual eye, looked forward to New York, Calcutta, Sidney Cove, across the ages and the oceans; and thought what Wellingtons, Washingtons, Shakspears, Miltons, Watts, Arkwrights, William Pitts and Davie Crocketts had to issue from that business, and do their several taskworks so,—*he* would have said, those leather-boats of Hengst's had a kind of cargo in them! A genealogic Mythus superior to any in the old Greek, to almost any in the old Hebrew itself; and not a Mythus either, but every fibre of it fact. An Epic Poem was there, and all manner of poems; except that the Poet has not yet made his appearance.'

'Six centuries of obscure endeavour,' continues Sauerteig, 'which to read Historians, you would incline to call mere obscure slaughter, discord, and misendeavour; of which all that the human memory, after a thousand readings, can remember, is that it resembled, what Milton names it, the " flocking and fighting of kites and crows:" this, in brief, is the history of the Heptarchy or Seven Kingdoms. Six centuries; a stormy spring-time, if there ever was one, for a Nation. Obscure fighting of kites and crows, however, was not the History of it; but was only what the dim Historians of it saw good to record. Were not forests felled, bogs drained, fields made arable, towns built, laws made, and the Thought and Practice of men in many ways perfected? Venerable Bede had got a language which he could now not only speak, but spell and put on paper: think what lies in that. Bemurmured by the German sea-flood swinging slow with sullen roar against those hoarse Northumbrian rocks, the venerable man set down several things in a legible manner. Or was the smith idle, hammering only war-tools? He had learned metallurgy, stithy-work in general; and made ploughshares withal, and adzes and mason-hammers. *Castra*, Caesters or Chesters, Dons, Tons (*Zauns*, Inclosures or *Towns*), not a few, did they not stand there; of burnt brick, of timber, of lath-and-clay; sending up the peaceable smoke of hearths? England had a History then too; though no Historian to write it. Those "flockings and fightings," sad inevitable necessities, were the expensive tentative steps towards some capability of living and working in concert: experiments they were, not always conclusive, to ascertain who had the might over whom, the right over whom.

'M. Thierry has written an ingenious Book, celebrating with considerable pathos the fate of the Saxons fallen under that fierce-hearted *Conquistator*, Acquirer or Conqueror, as he is named. M. Thierry professes to have a turn for looking at that side of things: the fate of the Welsh too moves him; of the Celts generally, whom a fiercer race swept before them into the mountainous nooks of the West, whither they were not worth following. Noble deeds, according to M. Thierry, were done by these unsuccessful men, heroic sufferings undergone; which it is a pious duty to rescue from forgetfulness. True, surely! A tear at least is due to the unhappy: it is right and fit that there should be a man to assert that lost cause too, and see what can still be made of it. Most right:—and yet, on the whole, taking matters on that great scale, what can we say but that the cause which pleased the gods has in the end to please Cato also? Cato cannot alter it; Cato will find that he cannot at bottom wish to alter it. Might and Right do differ frightfully from hour to hour; but give them centuries to try it in, they are found to be identical. Whose land *was* this of Britain? God's who made it, His and no other's it was and is. Who of God's creatures had right to live in it? The wolves and bisons? Yes they; till one with a better right shewed himself. The Celt, "aboriginal savage of Europe," as a snarling antiquary names him, arrived, pretending to have a better right; and did accordingly, not without pain to the bisons, make good the same. He had a better right to that piece of God's land; namely a better might to turn it to use;—a might to settle himself there, at least, and try what use he could turn it to. The bisons disappeared; the Celts took possession, and tilled. Forever, was it to be? Alas, *Forever* is not a category that can establish itself in this world of Time. A world of Time, by the very definition of it, is a world of mortality and mutability, of Beginning and Ending. No property is eternal but God the Maker's: whom Heaven permits to take possession, his is the right; Heaven's sanction *is* such permission, —while it lasts: nothing more can be said. Why does that hyssop grow there, in the chink of the wall? Because the whole universe, sufficiently occupied otherwise, could not hitherto prevent its growing! It has the might and the right. By the same great law do Roman Empires establish themselves, Christian Religions promulgate themselves, and all extant Powers bear rule. The strong thing is the just thing: this thou wilt find throughout in our world;—as indeed was God and Truth the Maker of our world, or was Satan and Falsehood?

'One proposition widely current as to this Norman Conquest is of a Physiologic sort: That the conquerors and conquered here were of different races; nay that the Nobility of England is still, to this hour, of a somewhat different blood from the commonalty, their fine Norman features contrasting so pleasantly with the coarse Saxon ones of the others. God knows, there are coarse enough features to be seen among the commonalty of that country; but if the Nobility's be finer, it is not their Normanhood that can be the reason. Does the above Physiologist reflect who those same Normans, Northmen, originally were? Baltic Saxons, and what other miscellany of Lurdanes, Jutes and Deutsch Pirates from the East-sea marshes would join them in plunder of France! If living three centuries longer in Heathenism, sea-robbery, and the unlucrative fishing of ambergris could ennoble them beyond the others, then were they ennobled. The Normans were Saxons who had learned to speak French. No: by Thor and Wodan, the Saxons were all as noble as needful;—shaped, says the Mythus, "from the rock of the Harzgebirge;" brother-tribes being made of clay, wood, water, or what other material might be going! A stubborn, taciturn, sulky, indomitable rock-made race of men; as the figure they cut in all quarters, in the cane-brake of Arkansas, in the Ghauts of the Himmalayha, no less than in London City, in Warwick or Lancaster County, does still abundantly manifest.'

'To this English People in World-History, there have been, shall I prophesy. Two grand tasks assigned? Huge-looming through the dim tumult of the always incommensurable Present Time, outlines of two tasks disclose themselves: the grand Industrial task of conquering some half or more of this Terraqueous Planet for the use of man; then secondly, the grand Constitutional task of sharing, in some pacific endurablemanner, the fruit of said conquest, and shewing all people how it might be done. These I will call their two tasks, discernible hitherto in World History: in both of these they have made respectable though unequal progress. Steamengines, ploughshares, pick-axes; what is meant by conquering this Planet, they partly know. Elective franchise, ballot-box, representative assembly; how to accomplish sharing of that conquest, they do not so well know. Europe knows not; Europe vehemently asks in these days, but receives no answer, no credible answer. For as to the partial Delolmish, Benthamee, or other French or English answers, current in the proper quarters and highly beneficial and indispensable there, thy disbelief in them as final answers, I take it, is complete.'

'Succession of rebellions? Successive clippings away of the Supreme Authority; class after class rising in revolt to say, "We will no more be governed so"? That is not the history of the English Constitution; not altogether that. Rebellion is the means, but it is not the motive cause. The motive cause, and true secret of the matter, were always this: The necessity there was for rebelling?

'Rights I will permit thee to call everywhere "correctly-articulated *mights*." A dreadful business to articulate correctly! Consider those Barons of Runnymead; consider all manner of successfully revolting men! Your Great Charter has to be experimented on, by battle and debate, for a hundred-and-fifty years; is then found to *be* correct; and stands as true *Magna Charta*—nigh cut in pieces by a tailor, short of measures, in later generations. Mights, I say, are a dreadful business to articulate correctly! Yet articulated they have to be; the time comes for it, the need comes for it, and with enormous difficulty and experimenting it is got done. Call it not succession of rebellions; call it rather succession of expansions, of enlightenments, gift of articulate utterance descending ever lower. Class after class acquires faculty of utterance,—Necessity teaching and compelling; as the dumb man, seeing the knife at his father's throat, suddenly acquired speech! Consider too how class after class not only acquires faculty of articulating what its might is, but likewise grows in might, acquires might or loses might; so that always, after a space, there is not only new gift of articulating, but there is something new to articulate. Constitutional epochs will never cease among men.'

'And so now, the Barons all settled and satisfied, a new class hitherto silent had begun to speak; the Middle Class, namely. In the time of James First, not only Knights of the Shire but Parliamentary Burgesses assemble; a real House of Commons has come decisively into play,—much to the astonishment of James First. We call it a growth of mights, if also of necessities; a growth of power to articulate mights, and make rights of them.

'In those past silent centuries, among those silent classes, much had been going on. Not only had red-deer in the New and other Forests been got preserved and shot; and treacheries of Simon de Montfort, wars of Red and White Roses, Battles of Crecy, Battles of Bosworth and many other battles been got transacted and adjusted; but England wholly, not without sore toil and aching bones to the millions of sires and the millions of sons these eighteen generations, had been got drained and tilled, covered with yellow harvests, beautiful and rich possessions; the mud-wooden Caesters and Chesters had become steepled tile-roofed compact Towns. Sheffield had taken to the manufacture of Sheffield whittles; Worstead could from wool spin yarn, and knit or weave the same into stockings or breeches for men. England had property valuable to the auctioneer; but the accumulate manufacturing, commercial, economic *skill* which lay impalpably warehoused in English hands and heads, what auctioneer could estimate?

'Hardly an Englishman to be met with but could *do* something; some cunninger thing than break his fellow-creature's head with battle-axes. The seven incorporated trades, with their million guild-brethren, with their hammers, their shuttles and tools, what an army;—fit to conquer the land of England, as we say, and to hold it conquered! Nay, strangest of all, the English people had acquired the faculty and habit of thinking,—even of believing: individual conscience had unfolded itself among them; Conscience, and Intelligence its handmaid. Ideas of innumerable kinds were circulating among these men: witness one Shakspeare, a woolcomber, poacher, or whatever else at Stratford in Warwickshire, who happened to write books! The finest human figure, as I apprehend, that Nature has hitherto seen fit to, make of our widely diffused Teutonic clay. Saxon, Norman, Celt or Sarmat, I find no human soul so beautiful, these fifteen hundred known years;—our supreme modern European man. Him England had contrived to realise: were there not ideas?

'Ideas poetic and also Puritanic,—that had to seek utterance in the notablest way! England had got her Shakspeare; but was now about to get her Milton and Oliver Cromwell. This too we will call a new expansion, hard as it might be to articulate and adjust; this, that a man could actually have a Conscience for his own behoof, and not for his Priest's only; that his Priest, be who he might, would henceforth have to take that fact along with him. One of the hardest things to adjust! It is not adjusted down to this hour. It lasts onwards to the time they call "Glorious Revolution" before so much as a reasonable truce can be made, and the war proceed by logic mainly. And still it is war, and no peace, unless we call waste vacancy peace. But it needed to be adjusted, as the others had done, as still others will do. Nobility at Runnymead cannot endure foul-play grown palpable; no more can Gentry in Long Parliament; no more can Commonalty in Parliament they name Reformed. Prynne's bloody ears were as a testimony and question to all England: "Englishmen, is this fair?" England, no longer continent of herself, answered, bellowing as with the voice of lions: "No, it is not fair!"'

'But now on the Industrial side, while this great Constitutional controversy, and revolt of the Middle Class had not ended, had yet but begun, what a shoot was that that England, carelessly, in quest of other objects, struck out across the Ocean, into the waste land which it named *New* England! Hail to thee, poor little ship Mayflower, of Delft-Haven: poor common-looking ship, hired by common charterparty for coined dollars; caulked with mere oakum and tar; provisioned with vulgarest biscuit and bacon;— yet what ship Argo, or miraculous epic ship built by the Sea-gods, was not a foolish bumbarge in comparison? Golden fleeces or the like these sailed for, with or without effect; thou little Mayflower hadst in thee a veritable Promethean spark; the life-spark of the largest Nation on our Earth,—so we may already name the Transatlantic Saxon Nation. They went seeking leave to hear sermon in their own method, these Mayflower Puritans; a most honest indispensable search: and yet, like Saul the son of Kish, seeking a small thing, they found this unexpected great thing! Honour to the brave and true; they verily, we say, carry fire from Heaven, and have a power that themselves dream not of. Let all men honour Puritanism, since God has so honoured it. Islam itself, with its wild heartfelt "*Allah, akbar,* God is great," was it not honoured? There is but one thing without honour; smitten with eternal barrenness, inability to do or be: Insincerity,

Unbelief. He who believes no *thing* who believes only the shows of things, is not in relation with Nature and Fact at all. Nature denies him; orders him at his earliest convenience to disappear. Let him disappear from her domains—into those of Chaos, Hypothesis and Simulacrum, or wherever else his parish may be.'

'As to the Third Constitutional controversy, that of the Working Classes, which now debates itself everywhere these fifty years, in France specifically since 1789, in England too since 1831, it is doubtless the hardest of all to get articulated: finis of peace, or even reasonable truce on this, is a thing I have little prospect of for several generations. Dark, wild-weltering, dreary, boundless; nothing heard on it yet but ballot-boxes. Parliamentary arguing; not to speak of much far worse arguing, by steel and lead, from Valmy to Waterloo, to Peterloo!'—

'And yet of Representative Assemblies may not this good be said: That contending parties in a country do thereby ascertain one another's strength? They fight there, since fight they must, by petition. Parliamentary eloquence, not by sword, bayonet and bursts of military cannon. Why do men fight at all, if it be not that they are yet *un*acquainted with one another's strength, and must fight and ascertain it? Knowing that thou art stronger than I, that thou canst compel me, I will submit to thee: unless I chance to prefer extermination, and slightly circuitous suicide, there is no other course for me. That in England, by public meetings, by petitions, by elections, leading-articles, and other jangling hubbub and tongue-fence which perpetually goes on everywhere in that country, people ascertain one another's strength, and the most obdurate House of Lords has to yield and give in before it come to cannonading and guillotinement: this is a saving characteristic of England. Nay, at bottom, is not this the celebrated English Constitution itself? This *un*spoken Constitution, whereof Privilege of Parliament, Money-Bill, Mutiny-Bill, and all that could be spoken and enacted hitherto, is not the essence and body, but only the shape and skin? Such Constitution is, in our times, verily invaluable.'

'Long stormy spring-time, wet contentious April, winter chilling the lap of very May; but at length the season of summer does come. So long the tree stood naked; angry wiry naked boughs moaning and creaking in the wind: you would say. Cut it down, why cumbereth it the ground? Not so; we must wait; all things will have their time.—Of the man Shakspeare, and his Elizabethan Era, with its Sydneys, Raleighs, Bacons, what could we say? That it was a spiritual flower-time. Suddenly, as with the breath of June, your rude naked tree is touched; bursts into leaves and flowers, *such* leaves and flowers. The past long ages of nakedness, and wintry fermentation and elaboration, have done their part, though seeming to do nothing. The past silence has got a voice, all the more significant the longer it had continued silent. In trees, men, institutions, creeds, nations, in all things extant and growing in this universe, we may note such vicissitudes, and budding-times. Moreover there are spiritual budding-times; and then also there are physical, appointed to nations.

'Thus in the middle of that poor calumniated Eighteenth Century, see once more! Long winter again past, the dead-seeming tree proves to be living, to have been always living; after motionless times, every bough shoots forth on the sudden, very strangely:—it now turns out that this favoured England was not only to have had her Shakspeares, Bacons, Sydneys, but to have her Watts, Arkwrights, Brindleys! We will honour greatness in all kinds. The Prospero evoked the singing of Ariel, and took captive the world with those melodies: the same Prospero can send his Fire-demons panting across all oceans; shooting with the speed of meteors, on cunning highways, from end to end of kingdoms; and make Iron his missionary, preaching *its*evangel to the brute Primeval Powers, which listen and obey: neither is this small. Manchester, with its cotton-fuz, its smoke and dust, its tumult and contentious squalor, is hideous to thee? Think not so: a precious substance, beautiful as magic dreams and yet no dream but a reality, lies hidden in that noisome wrappage;—a wrappage struggling indeed (look at Chartisms and such like) to cast itself off, and leave the beauty free and visible there! Hast thou heard, with sound ears, the awakening of a Manchester, on Monday morning, at half-past five by the clock; the rushing off of its thousand mills, like the boom of an Atlantic tide, ten thousand times ten thousand spools and spindles all set humming there,—it is perhaps, if thou knew it well, sublime as a Niagara, or more so. Cotton-spinning is the clothing of the naked in its result; the triumph of man over matter in its means. Soot and despair are not the essence of it; they are divisible from it,—at this hour, are they not crying fiercely to be divided? The great Goethe, looking at cotton Switzerland, declared it, I am told, to be of all things that he had seen in this world the most poetical. Whereat friend Kanzler von Müller, in search of the palpable picturesque, could not but stare wide-eyed. Nevertheless our World-Poet knew well what he was saying.'

'Richard Arkwright, it would seem, was not a beautiful man; no romance-hero with haughty eyes, Apollo-lip, and gesture like the herald Mercury; a plain almost gross, bag-cheeked, potbellied Lancashire man, with an air of painful reflection, yet also of copious free digestion;—a man stationed by the community to shave certain dusty beards, in the Northern parts of England, at a halfpenny each. To such end, we say, by forethought, oversight, accident and arrangement, had Richard Arkwright been, by the community of England and his own consent, set apart. Nevertheless, in strapping of razors, in lathering of dusty beards, and the contradictions and confusions attendant thereon, the man had notions in that rough head of his; spindles, shuttles, wheels and contrivances plying ideally within the same: rather hopeless-looking; which, however, he did at last bring to bear. Not without difficulty! His townsfolk rose in mob round him, for threatening to shorten labour, to shorten wages; so that he had to fly, with broken washpots, scattered household, and seek refuge elsewhere. Nay his wife too, as I learn, rebelled; burnt his wooden model of his spinning-wheel; resolute that he should stick to his razors rather;—for which, however, he decisively, as thou wilt rejoice to understand, packed her out of doors. O reader, what a Historical Phenomenon is that bag-cheeked, potbellied, much-enduring, much-inventing barber! French Revolutions were abrewing: to resist the same in any measure, imperial Kaisers were impotent without the cotton and cloth of England; and it was this man that had to give England the power of cotton.'

'Neither had Watt of the Steamengine a heroic origin, any kindred with the princes of this world. The princes of this world were shooting their partridges; noisily, in Parliament or elsewhere, solving the question. Head or tail? while this man with blackened fingers, with grim brow, was searching out, in his workshop, the Fire-secret; or, having found it, was painfully wending to and fro in quest of a "monied man," as indispensable man-midwife of the same. Reader, thou shalt admire what is admirable, not what is dressed in admirable; learn to know the British lion even when he is not throne-supporter, and also the British jackass in lion's skin even when he is. Ah, couldst thou always, what a world were it! But has the Berlin Royal Academy or any English Useful-Knowledge Society discovered, for instance, who it was that first scratched earth with a stick; and threw *corns*, the biggest he could find, into it; seedgrains of a certain grass, which he named *white or wheat?* Again, what is the whole Tees-water and other breeding-world to him who stole home from the forests the first bison-calf, and bred it up to be a tame bison, a milk-cow? No machine of all they shewed me in Birmingham can be put in comparison for ingenuity with that figure of the wedge named *knife*, of the wedges named *saw* of the lever named *hammer*:—nay is it not with the hammer-knife, named *sword*, that men fight, and maintain any semblance of constituted authority that yet survives among us? The steamengine I call fire-demon and great; but it is nothing to the invention of *fire*, Prometheus, Tubalcain, Triptolemus! Are not our greatest men as good as lost? The men that walk daily among us, clothing us, warming us, feeding us, walk shrouded in darkness, mere mythic men.

'It is said, ideas produce revolutions; and truly so they do; not spiritual ideas only, but even mechanical. In this clanging clashing universal Sword-dance that the European world now dances for the last half-century, Voltaire is but one choragus, where Richard Arkwright is another. Let it dance itself out. When Arkwright shall have become mythic like Arachne, we shall still spin in peaceable profit by him; and the Sword-dance, with all its sorrowful shufflings, Waterloo waltzes, Moscow gallopades, how forgotten will that be!'

'On the whole, were not all these things most unexpected, unforeseen? As indeed what thing is foreseen; especially what man, the parent of things! Robert Clive in that same time went out, with a developed gift of penmanship, as writer or superior book-keeper to a trading factory established in the distant East. With gift of penmanship developed; with other gifts not yet developed, which the calls of the case did by and by develope. Not fit for book-keeping alone, the man was found fit for conquering Nawaubs, founding kingdoms, Indian Empires! In a questionable manner, Indian Empire from the other hemisphere took up its abode in Leadenhall Street, in the City of London.

'Accidental all these things and persons look, unexpected every one of them to man. Yet inevitable every one of them; foreseen, not unexpected, by Supreme Power; prepared, appointed from afar. Advancing always through all centuries, in the middle of the eighteenth they *arrived*. The Saxon kindred burst forth into cotton-spinning, cloth-cropping, iron-forging, steamengining, railwaying, commercing and careering towards all the winds of Heaven,—in this inexplicable noisy manner; the noise of which, in Power-mills, in progress-of-the-species Magazines, still deafens us somewhat. Most noisy, sudden! The Staffordshire coal-stratum, and coal-strata, lay side by side with iron-strata, quiet since the creation of the world. Water flowed in Lancashire and Lanarkshire; bituminous fire lay bedded in rocks there too,—over which how many fighting Stanleys, black Douglases, and other the like contentious persons, had fought out their bickerings and broils, not without result, we will hope! But God said. Let the iron missionaries be; and they were. Coal and iron, so long close unregardful neighbours, are wedded together; Birmingham and Wolverhampton, and the hundred Stygian forges, with their firethroats and never-resting sledge-hammers, rose into day. Wet Manconium stretched out her hand towards Carolina and the torrid zone, and plucked cotton there: who could forbid her, her that had the skill to weave it? Fish fled thereupon from the Mersey

River, vexed with innumerable keels. England, I say, dug out her bitumen-fire, and bade it work: towns rose, and steeple-chimneys; —Chartisms also, and Parliaments they name Reformed.'

Such, figuratively given, are some prominent points, chief mountain-summits, of our English History past and present, according to the Author of this strange untranslated Work, whom we think we recognise to be an old acquaintance.

CHAPTER IX.
PARLIAMENTARY RADICALISM.

To us, looking at these matters somewhat in the same light, Reform-Bills, French Revolutions, Louis-Philippes. Chartisms, Revolts of Three Days, and what not, are no longer inexplicable. Where the great mass of men is tolerably right, all is right; where they are not right, all is wrong. The speaking classes speak and debate, each for itself; the great dumb, deep-buried class lies like an Enceladus, who in his pain, if he will complain of it, has to produce earthquakes! Everywhere, in these countries, in these times, the central fact worthy of all consideration forces itself on us in this shape: the claim of the Free Working-man to be raised to a level, we may say, with the Working Slave; his anger and cureless discontent till that be done. Food, shelter, due guidance, in return for his labour: candidly interpreted. Chartism and all such *isms* mean that; and the madder they are, do they not the more emphatically mean, "See what guidance you have given us? What delirium we are brought to talk and project, guided by nobody?" *Laissez-faire* on the part of the Governing Classes, we repeat again and again, will, with whatever difficulty, have to cease; pacific mutual division of the spoil, and a world well let alone, will no longer suffice. A Do-nothing Guidance; and it is a Do-something World! Would to God our Ducal *Duces* would become Leaders indeed; our Aristocracies and Priesthoods discover in some suitable degree what the world expected of them, what the world could no longer do without getting of them! Nameless unmeasured confusions, misery to themselves and us, might so be spared. But that too will be as God has appointed. If they learn, it will be well and happy: if not they, then others instead of them will and must, and once more, though after a long sad circuit, it will be well and happy.

Neither is the history of Chartism mysterious in these times; especially if that of Radicalism be looked at. All along, for the last five-and-twenty years, it was curious to note how the internal discontent of England struggled to find vent for itself through *any* orifice: the poor patient, all sick from centre to surface, complains now of this member, now of that;—corn-laws, currency-laws, free-trade, protection, want of free-trade: the poor patient tossing from side to side, seeking a sound side to lie on, finds none. This Doctor says, it is the liver; that other, it is the lungs, the head, the heart, defective transpiration in the skin. A thoroughgoing Doctor of eminence said, it was rotten boroughs; the want of extended suffrage to destroy rotten boroughs. From of old, the English patient himself had a continually recurring notion that this was it. The English people are used to suffrage; it is their panacea for all that goes wrong with them; they have a fixed-idea of suffrage. Singular enough: one's right to vote for a Member of Parliament, to send one's 'twenty-thousandth part of a master of tongue-fence to National Palaver,'—the Doctors asserted that this was Freedom, this and no other. It seemed credible to many men, of high degree and of low. The persuasion of remedy grew, the evil was pressing; Swing's ricks were on fire. Some nine years ago, a State-surgeon rose, and in peculiar circumstances said: let there be extension of the suffrage; let the great Doctor's nostrum, the patient's old passionate prayer be fulfilled!

Parliamentary Radicalism, while it gave articulate utterance to the discontent of the English people, could not by its worst enemy be said to be without a function. If it is in the natural order of things that there must be discontent, no less so is it that such discontent should have an outlet, a Parliamentary voice. Here the matter is debated of, demonstrated, contradicted, qualified, reduced to feasibility;—can at least solace itself with hope, and die gently, convinced of *un*feasibility. The New, Untried ascertains how it will fit itself into the arrangements of the Old; whether the Old can be compelled to admit it; how in that case it may, with the minimum of violence, be admitted. Nor let us count it an easy one, this function of Radicalism; it was one of the most difficult. The pain-stricken patient does, indeed, without effort groan and complain; but not without effort does the physician ascertain what it is that has gone wrong with him, how some remedy may be devised for him. And above all, if your patient is not one sick man, but a whole sick nation! Dingy dumb millions, grimed with dust and sweat, with darkness, rage and sorrow, stood round these men, saying, or struggling as they could to say: "Behold, our lot is unfair; our life is not whole but sick; we cannot live under injustice; go ye and get us justice!" For whether the poor operative clamoured for Time-bill, Factory-bill, Corn-bill, for or against whatever bill, this was what he meant. All bills plausibly presented might have some look of hope in them, might get some clamour of approval from him; as, for the man wholly sick, there is no disease in the Nosology but he can trace in himself some symptoms of it. Such was the mission of Parliamentary Radicalism.

How Parliamentary Radicalism has fulfilled this mission, entrusted to its management these eight years now, is known to all men. The expectant millions have sat at a feast of the Barmecide; been bidden fill themselves with the imagination of meat. What thing has Radicalism obtained for them; what other than shadows of things has it so much as asked for them? Cheap Justice, Justice to Ireland, Irish Appropriation-Clause, Ratepaying Clause, Poor-Rate, Church-Rate, Household Suffrage, Ballot-Question 'open' or shut: not things but shadows of things; Benthamee formulas; barren as the east-wind! An Ultra-radical, not seemingly of the Benthamee species, is forced to exclaim: 'The people are at last wearied. They say. Why should we be ruined in our shops, thrown out of our farms, voting for these men? Ministerial majorities decline; this Ministry has become impotent, had it even the will to do good. They have called long to us, "We are a Reform Ministry; will ye not support *us?*" We have supported them; borne them forward indignantly on our shoulders, time after time, fall after fall, when they had been hurled out into the street; and lay prostrate, helpless, like dead luggage. It is the fact of a Reform Ministry, not the name of one that we would support!Languor, sickness of hope deferred pervades the public mind; the public mind says at last, Why all this struggle for the *name* of a Reform Ministry? Let the Tories be Ministry if they will; let at least some living reality be Ministry! A rearing horse that will only run backward, he is not the horse one would choose to travel on: yet of all conceivable horses the worst is the dead horse. Mounted on a rearing horse, you may back him, spur him, check him, make a little way even backwards: but seated astride of your dead horse, what chance is there for you in the chapter of possibilities? You sit motionless, hopeless, a spectacle to gods and men.'

There is a class of revolutionists named *Girondins*, whose fate in history is remarkable enough! Men who rebel, and urge the Lower Classes to rebel, ought to have other than Formulas to go upon. Men who discern in the misery of the toiling complaining millions not misery, but only a raw-material which can be wrought upon, and traded in, for one's own poor hidebound theories and egoisms; to whom millions of living fellow-creatures, with beating hearts in their bosoms, beating, suffering, hoping, are 'masses,' mere 'explosive masses for blowing down Bastilles with,' for voting at hustings for *us:* such men are of the questionable species! No man is justified in resisting by word or deed the Authority he lives under, for a light cause, be such Authority what it may. Obedience, little as many may consider that side of the matter, is the primary duty of man. No man but is bound indefeasibly, with all force of obligation, to obey. Parents, teachers, superiors, leaders, these all creatures recognise as deserving obedience. Recognised or not recognised, a man *has* his superiors, a regular hierarchy above him; extending up, degree above degree; to Heaven itself and God the Maker, who made His world not for anarchy but for rule and order! It is not a light matter when the just man can recognise in the powers set over him no longer anything that is divine; when resistance against such becomes a deeper law of order than obedience to them; when the just man sees himself in the tragical position of a stirrer up of strife! Rebel, without due and most due cause, is the ugliest of words; the first rebel was Satan.—

But now in these circumstances shall we blame the unvoting disappointed millions that they turn away with horror from this name of a Reform Ministry, name of a Parliamentary Radicalism, and demand a fact and reality thereof? That they too, having still faith in what so many had faith in, still count 'extension of the suffrage' the one thing needful; and say, in such manner as they can. Let the suffrage be still extended,*then* all will be well? It is the ancient British faith; promulgated in these ages by prophets and evangelists; preached forth from barrel-heads by all manner of men. He who is free and blessed has his twenty-thousandth part of a master of tongue-fence in National Palaver; whosoever is not blessed but unhappy, the ailment of him is that he has it not. Ought he not to have it then? By the law of God and of men, yea; —and will have it withal! Chartism, with its 'five points,' borne aloft on pikeheads and torchlight meetings, is there. Chartism is one of the most natural phenomena in England. Not that Chartism now exists should provoke wonder; but that the invited hungry people should have sat eight years at such table of the Barmecide, patiently expecting somewhat from the Name of a

Reform Ministry, and not till after eight years have grown hopeless, this is the respectable side of the miracle.

CHAPTER X.

IMPOSSIBLE.

'BUT what are we to do?" exclaims the practical man, impatiently on every side: "Descend from speculation and the safe pulpit, down into the rough market-place, and say what can be done?"— O practical man, there seem very many things which practice and true manlike effort, in Parliament and out of it, might actually avail to do. But the first of all things, as already said, is to gird thyself up for actual doing; to know that thou actually either must do, or, as the Irish say, 'come out of that!'

It is not a lucky word this same *impossible*: no good comes of those that have it so often in their mouth. Who is he that says always, There is a lion in the way? Sluggard, thou must slay the lion then; the way has to be travelled! In Art, in Practice, innumerable critics will demonstrate that most things are henceforth impossible; that we are got, once for all, into the region of perennial commonplace, and must contentedly continue there. Let such critics demonstrate; it is the nature of them: what harm is in it? Poetry once well demonstrated to be impossible, arises the Burns, arises the Goethe. Unheroic commonplace being now clearly all we have to look for, comes the Napoleon, comes the conquest of the world. It was proved by fluxionary calculus, that steamships could never get across from the farthest point of Ireland to the nearest of Newfoundland: impelling force, resisting force, maximum here, minimum there; by law of Nature, and geometric demonstration:—what could be done? The Great Western could weigh anchor from Bristol Port; that could be done. The Great Western, bounding safe through the gullets of the Hudson, threw her cable out on the capstan of New York, and left our still moist paper-demonstration to dry itself at leisure. "Impossible?" cried Mirabeau to his secretary, "*Ne me dites jamais ce bête de mot*, Never name to me that blockhead of a word!"

There is a phenomenon which one might call Paralytic Radicalism, in these days; which gauges with Statistic measuring-reed, sounds with Philosophic Politico-Economic plummet the deep dark sea of troubles; and having taught us rightly what an infinite sea of troubles it is, sums up with the practical inference, and use of consolation. That nothing whatever can be done in it by man, who has simply to sit still, and look wistfully to 'time and general laws;' and thereupon, without so much as recommending suicide, coldly takes its leave of us. Most paralytic, uninstructive; unproductive of any comfort to one! They are an unreasonable class who cry, "Peace, peace,"when there *is* no peace. But what kind of class are they who cry, "Peace, peace, have I not *told you* that there is no peace?" Paralytic Radicalism, frequent among those Statistic friends of ours, is one of the most afflictive phenomena the mind of man can be called to contemplate. One prays that *it* at least might cease. Let Paralysis retire into secret places, and dormitories proper for it; the public highways ought not to be occupied by people demonstrating that motion is impossible. Paralytic;—and also, thank Heaven, entirely false! Listen to a thinker of another sort: 'All evil, and this evil too, is as a nightmare; the instant you begin to *stir* under it, the *evil* is, properly speaking, gone.' Consider, O reader, whether it be not actually so? Evil, once manfully fronted, ceases to be evil; there is generous battle-hope in place of dead passive misery; the evil itself has become a kind of good.

To the practical man, therefore, we will repeat that he has, as the first thing he can 'do,' to gird himself up for actual doing; to know well that he is either there to do, or not there at all. Once rightly girded up, how many things will present themselves as doable which now are not attemptible! Two things, great things, dwell, for the last ten years, in all thinking heads in England; and are hovering, of late, even on the tongues of not a few. With a word on each of these, we will dismiss the practical man, and right gladly take ourselves into obscurity and silence again. Universal Education is the first great thing we mean; general Emigration is the second.

Who would suppose that Education were a thing which had to be advocated on the ground of local expediency, or indeed on any ground? As if it stood not on the basis of everlasting duty, as a prime necessity of man. It is a thing that should need no advocating; much as it does actually need. To impart the gift of thinking to those who cannot think, and yet who could in that case think: this, one would imagine, was the first function a government had to set about discharging. Were it not a cruel thing to see, in any province of an empire, the inhabitants living all mutilated in their limbs, each strong man with is right-arm lamed? How much crueller to find the strong soul, with its eyes still sealed, its eyes extinct so that it sees not! Light has come into the world, but to this poor peasant it has come in vain. For six thousand years the Sons of Adam, in sleepless effort, have been devising, doing, discovering; in mysterious infinite indissoluble communion, warring, a little band of brothers, against the great black empire of Necessity and Night; they have accomplished such a conquest and conquests: and to this man it is all as if it had not been. The four-and-twenty letters of the Alphabet are still Runic enigmas to him. He passes by on the other side; and that great Spiritual Kingdom, the toilwon conquest of his own brothers, all that his brothers have conquered, is a thing nonextant for him. An invisible empire; he knows it not, suspects it not. And is it not his withal; the conquest of his own brothers, the lawfully acquired possession of all men? Baleful enchantment lies over him, from generation to generation; he knows not that such an empire is his, that such an empire is at all. O, what are bills of rights, emancipations of black slaves into black apprentices, lawsuits in chancery for some short usufruct of a bit of land? The grand 'seedfield of Time' is this man's, and you give it him not. Time's seedfield, which includes the Earth and all her seedfields and pearl-oceans, nay her sowers too and pearl-divers, all that was wise and heroic and victorious here below; of which the Earth's centuries are but as furrows, for it stretches forth from the Beginning onward even into this Day!

'My inheritance, how lordly wide and fair;
 Time is my fair seedfield, to Time I'm heir!'

Heavier wrong is not done under the sun. It lasts from year to year, from century to century; the blinded sire slaves himself out, and leaves a blinded son; and men, made in the image of God, continue as two-legged beasts of labour;—and in the largest empire of the world, it is a debate whether a small fraction of the Revenue of one Day (30,000*l.* is but that) shall, after Thirteen Centuries, be laid out on it, or not laid out on it. Have we Governors, have we Teachers; have we had a Church these thirteen hundred years? What is an Overseer of souls, an Archoverseer, Archiepiscopus? Is he something? If so, let him lay his hand on his heart, and say what thing!

But quitting all that, of which the human soul cannot well speak in terms of civility, let us observe now that Education is not only an eternal duty, but has at length become even a temporary and ephemeral one, which the necessities of the hour will oblige us to look after. These Twenty-four million labouring men, if their affairs remain unregulated, chaotic, will burn ricks and mills; reduce us, themselves and the world into ashes and ruin. Simply their affairs cannot remain unregulated, chaotic; but must be regulated, brought into some kind of order. What intellect were able to regulate them? The intellect of a Bacon, the energy of a Luther, if left to their own strength, might pause in dismay before such a task; a Bacon and Luther added together, to be perpetual prime minister over us, could not do it. No one great and greatest intellect can do it. What can? Only Twenty-four million ordinary intellects, once awakened into action; these, well presided over, may. Intellect, insight, is the discernment of order in disorder; it is the discovery of the will of Nature, of God's will; the beginning of the capability to walk according to that. With perfect intellect, were such possible without perfect morality, the world would be perfect; its efforts unerringly correct, its results continually successful, its condition faultless. Intellect is like light; the Chaos becomes a World under it: *fiat lux*. These Twenty-four million intellects are but common intellects; but they are intellects; in earnest about the matter, instructed each about his own province of it; labouring each perpetually, with what partial light can be attained, to bring such province into rationality. From the partial determinations and their conflict, springs the universal. Precisely what quantity of intellect was in the Twenty-four millions will be exhibited by the result they arrive at; that quantity and no more. According as there was intellect or no intellect in the individuals, will the general conclusion they make out embody itself as a world-healing Truth and Wisdom, or as a baseless fateful Hallucination, a Chimæra breathing *not* fabulous fire!

Dissenters call for one scheme of Education, the Church objects; this party objects, and that; there is endless objection, by him and by her and by it: a subject encumbered with difficulties on every side! Pity that difficulties exist; that Religion, of all things, should occasion difficulties. We do not extenuate them: in their reality they are considerable; in their appearance and pretension, they are insuperable, heart-appalling to all Secretaries of the Home Department. For, in very truth, how can Religion be divorced from Education? An irreverent knowledge is no knowledge; may be a development of the logical or other handicraft faculty inward or outward; but is no culture of the soul of a man. A knowledge that ends in barren self-worship, comparative indifference or contempt for all God's Universe except one insignificant item thereof, what is it? Handicraft development, and even shallow as handicraft. Nevertheless is handicraft itself, and the habit of the merest logic, nothing? It is already something; it is the indispensable beginning of every thing! Wise men know it to be an indispensable something; not yet much; and would so gladly superadd to it the element whereby it may become all. Wise men would not quarrel in attempting this; they would lovingly co-operate in attempting it.

'And now how teach religion?' so asks the indignant Ultra-radical, cited above; an Ultra-radical seemingly not of the Benthamee species, with whom, though his dialect is far different, there are sound Churchmen, we hope, who have some fellow-feeling: 'How teach religion? By plying with liturgies, catechisms, credos; droning thirty-nine or other articles incessantly into the infant ear? Friends! In that case, why not apply to Birmingham, and have Machines made, and set up at all street-corners, in highways and byways, to repeat and vociferate the same, not ceasing night or day? The genius of Birmingham is adequate to that. Albertus Magnus had a leather man that could articulate; not to speak of Martinus Scriblerus' Nürnberg man that could reason as well as we know who! Depend upon it, Birmingham can make machines to repeat liturgies and article; to do whatsoever feat is mechanical. And what were all schoolmasters, nay all priests and churches compared with this Birmingham Iron Church! Votes of two millions in aid of the church were then something. You order, at so many pounds a-head, so many thousand iron parsons as your grant covers; and fix them by satisfactory masonry in all quarters wheresoever wanted, to preach there independent of the world. In loud thoroughfares, still more in unawakened districts, troubled with argumentative infidelity, you make the windpipes wider, strengthen the main steam-cylinder; your parson preaches, to the due pitch, while you give him coal; and fears no man or thing. Here *were* a 'Church-extension;' to which I, with my last penny, did I believe in it, would subscribe.——Ye blind leaders of the blind! Are we Calmucks, that pray by turning of a rotatory calebash with written prayers in it? Is Mammon and machinery the means of converting human souls, as of spinning cotton? Is God, as Jean Paul predicted it would be, become verily a Force; the Æther too a Gas! Alas, that Atheism should have got the length of putting on priests' vestments, and penetrating into the sanctuary itself! Can dronings of articles, repetitions of liturgies, and all the cash andcontrivance of Birmingham and the Bank of England united bring ethereal fire into a human soul, quicken it out of earthly darkness into heavenly wisdom? Soul is kindled only by soul. To "teach" religion, the first thing needful, and also the last and the only thing, is finding of a man who *has* religion. All else follows from this, church-building, church-extension, whatever else is needful follows; without this nothing will follow.'

From which we for our part conclude that the method of teaching religion to the English people is still far behindhand; that the wise and pious may well ask themselves in silence wistfully, "How *is* that last priceless element, by which education becomes perfect, to be superadded?" and the unwise who think themselves pious, answering aloud, "By this method. By that method," long argue of it to small purpose.

But now, in the mean time, could not by some fit official person, some fit announcement be made, in words well-weighed, in plan well-schemed, adequately representing the facts of the thing. That after thirteen centuries of waiting, he the official person, and England with him, was minded now to have the mystery of the Alphabetic Letters imparted to all human souls in this realm? Teaching of religion was a thing he could not undertake to settle this day; it would be work for a day after this; the work of this day was teaching of the alphabet to all people. The miraculous art of reading and writing, such seemed to him the needful preliminary of all teaching, the first corner-stone of what foundation soever could be laid for what edifice soever, in the teaching kind. Let pious Churchism make haste, let pious Dissenterism make haste, let all pious preachers and missionaries make haste, bestir themselves according to their zeal and skill: he the official person stood up for the Alphabet; and was even impatient for it, having waited thirteen centuries now. He insisted, and would take no denial, postponement, promise, excuse or subterfuge, That all

English persons should be taught to read. He appealed to all rational Englishmen, of all creeds, classes and colours. Whether this was not a fair demand; nay whether it was not an indispensable one in these days, Swing and Chartism having risen? For a choice of inoffensive Hornbooks, and Schoolmasters able to teach reading, he trusted the mere secular sagacity of a National Collective Wisdom, in proper committee, might be found sufficient. He purposed to appoint such Schoolmasters, to venture on the choice of such Hornbooks; to send a Schoolmaster and Hornbook into every township, parish and hamlet of England; so that, in ten years hence, an Englishman who could not read might be acknowledged as the monster, which he really is!

This official person's plan we do not give. The *thing* lies there, with the facts of it, and with the appearances or sham-facts of it; a plan adequately representing the facts of the thing could by human energy be struck out, does lie there for discovery and striking out. It is his, the official person's duty, not ours, to mature a plan. We can believe that Churchism and Dissenterism would clamour aloud; but yet that in the mere secular Wisdom of Parliament a perspicacity equal to the choice of Hornbooks might, in very deed, be found to reside. England we believe would, if consulted, resolve to that effect. Alas, grants of a half-day's revenue once in the thirteen centuries for such an object, do not call out the voice of England, only the superficial clamour of England! Hornbooks unexceptionable to the candid portion of England, we will believe, might be selected. Nay, we can conceive that Schoolmasters fit to teach reading might, by a board of rational men, whether from Oxford or Hoxton, or from both or neither of these places, be pitched upon. We can conceive even, as in Prussia, that a penalty, civil disabilities, that penalties and disabilities till they were found effectual, might be by law inflicted on every parent who did not teach his children to read, on every man who had not been taught to read. We can conceive in fine, such is the vigour of our imagination, there might be found in England, at a dead-lift, strength enough to perform this miracle, and produce it henceforth as a miracle done: the teaching of England to read! Harder things, we do know, have been performed by nations before now, not abler-looking than England. Ah me! if, by some beneficent chance, there should be an official man found in England who could and would, with deliberate courage, after ripe counsel, with candid insight, with patience, practical sense, knowing realities to be real, knowing clamours to be clamorous and to seem real, propose this thing, and the innumerable things springing from it,—wo to any Churchism or any Dissenterism that cast itself athwart the path of that man! Avaunt ye gainsayers! is darkness and ignorance of the Alphabet necessary for you? Reconcile yourselves to the Alphabet, or depart elsewhither!—Would not all that has genuineness in England gradually rally round such a man; all that has strength in England? For realities alone have strength; wind-bags are wind; cant is cant, leave it alone there. Nor are all clamours momentous: among living creatures, we find, the loudest is the longest-eared; among lifeless things the loudest is the drum, the emptiest Alas, that official persons, and all of us, had not eyes to see what was real, what was merely chimerical, and thought or called itself real! How many dread minatory Castle-spectres should we leave there, with their admonishing right-hand and ghastly-burning saucer-eyes, to do simply whatsoever they might find themselves able to do! Alas, that we were not real ourselves; we should otherwise have surer vision for the real. Castle-spectres, in their utmost terror, are but poor mimicries of that real and most real terror which lies in the Life of every Man: that, thou coward, is the thing to be afraid of, if thou wilt live in fear. It is but the scratch of a bare bodkin; it is but the flight of a few days of time; and even thou, poor palpitating featherbrain, wilt find how real it is. ETERNITY: hast thou heard of that? Is that a fact, or is it no fact? Are Buckingham House and St. Stephens in that, or not in that?

But now we have to speak of the second great thing: Emigration. It was said above, all new epochs, so convulsed and tumultuous to look upon, are 'expansions,' increase of faculty not yet organised. It is eminently true of the confusions of this time of ours. Disorganic Manchester afflicts us with its Chartisms;yet is not spinning of clothes for the naked intrinsically a most blessed thing? Manchester once organic will bless and not afflict. The confusions, if we would understand them, are at bottom mere increase which we know not yet how to manage; 'new wealth which the old coffers will not hold.' How true is this, above all, of the strange phenomenon called *over-population!' Over-population is the grand anomaly, which is bringing all other anomalies to a crisis. Now once more, as at the end of the Roman Empire, a most confused epoch and yet one of the greatest, the Teutonic Countries find themselves too full. On a certain western rim of our small Europe, there are more men than were expected. Heaped up against the western shore there, and for a couple of hundred miles inward, the 'tide of population' swells too high, and confuses itself somewhat! Over-population? And yet, if this small western rim of Europe is overpeopled, does not everywhere else a whole vacant Earth, as it were, call to us. Come and till me, come and reap me! Can it be an evil that in an Earth such as ours there should be new Men? Considered as mercantile commodities, as working machines, is there in Birmingham or out of it a machine of such value? 'Good Heavens! a white European Man, standing on his two legs, with his two five-fingered Hands at his shackle-bones, and miraculous Head on his shoulders, is worth something considerable, one would say!' The stupid black African man brings money in the market; the much stupider four-footed horse brings money:—it is we that have not yet learned the art of managing our white European man!

The controversies on Malthus and the 'Population Principle,' 'Preventive check' and so forth, with which the public ear has been deafened for a long while, are indeed sufficiently mournful. Dreary, stolid, dismal, without hope for this world or the next, is all that of the preventive check and the denial of the preventive check. Anti-Malthusians quoting their Bible against palpable facts, are not a pleasant spectacle. On the other hand, how often have we read in Malthusian benefactors of the species: 'The working people have their condition in their own hands; let them diminish the supply of labourers, and of course the demand and the remuneration will increase!' Yes, let *them* diminish the supply: but who are they? They are twenty-four millions of human individuals, scattered over a hundred and eighteen thousand square miles of space and more; weaving, delving, hammering, joinering; each unknown to his neighbour; each distinct within his own skin. *They* are not a kind of character that can take a resolution, and act on it, very readily. Smart Sally in our alley proves all-too fascinating to brisk Tom in yours: can Tom be called on to make pause, and calculate the demand for labour in the British Empire first? Nay, if Tom did renounce his highest blessedness of life, and struggle and conquer like a Saint Francis of

Assisi, what would it profit him or us? Seven millions of the finest peasantry do not renounce, but proceed all the more briskly; and with blue-visaged Hibernians instead of fair Saxon Tomsons and Sallysons, the latter end of that country is worse than the beginning. O wonderful Malthusian prophets! Millenniums are undoubtedly coming, must come one way or the other: but will it be, think you, by twenty millions of working people simultaneously striking work in that department; passing, in universal trades-union, a resolution not to beget any more till the labour-market become satisfactory? By Day and Night! they were indeed irresistible so; not to be compelled by law or war; might make their own terms with the richer classes, and defy the world!

A shade more rational is that of those other benefactors of the species, who counsel that in each parish, in some central locality, instead of the Parish Clergyman, there might be established some Parish Exterminator; or say a Reservoir of Arsenic, kept up at the public expense, free to all parishioners; for *which*Church the rates probably would not be grudged.—Ah, it is bitter jesting on such a subject. One's heart is sick to look at the dreary chaos, and valley of Jehosaphat, scattered with the limbs and souls of one's fellow-men; and no divine voice, only creaking of hungry vultures, inarticulate bodeful ravens, horn-eyed parrots that do articulate, proclaiming. Let these bones live!—Dante's *Divina Commedia* is called the mournfullest of books: transcendent mistemper of the noblest soul; utterance of a boundless, godlike, unspeakable, implacable sorrow and protest against the world. But in Holywell Street, not long ago, we bought, for three-pence, a book still mournfuller: the Pamphlet of one "Marcus," whom his poor Chartist editor and republisher calls the "Demon Author." This *Marcus* Pamphlet was the book alluded to by Stephens the Preacher Chartist, in one of his harangues: it proves to be no fable that such a book existed; here it lies, 'Printed by John Hill, Black-horse Court, Fleet Street, and now reprinted for the instruction of the labourer, by William Dugdale, Holywell Street, Strand,' the exasperated Chartist editor who sells it you for three-pence. We have read Marcus; but his sorrow is not divine. We hoped he would turn out to have been in sport: ah no, it is grim earnest with him; grim as very death. Marcus is not a demon author at all: he is a benefactor of the species in his own kind; has looked intensely on the world's woes, from a Benthamee Malthusian watchtower, under a Heaven dead as iron; and does now, with much longwindedness, in a drawling, snuffling, circuitous, extremely dull, yet at bottom handfast and positive manner, recommend that all children of working people, after the third, be disposed of by 'painless extinction.' Charcoal-vapour and other methods exist. The mothers would consent, might be made to consent. Three children might be left living; or perhaps, for Marcus's calculations are not yet perfect, two and a half. There might be 'beautiful cemeteries with colonnades and flower-plots,' in which the patriot infanticide matrons might delight to take their evening walk of contemplation; and reflect what patriotesses they were, what a cheerful flowery world it was. Such is the scheme of Marcus; this is what he, for his share, could devise to heal the world's woes. A benefactor of the species, clearly recognisable as such: the saddest scientific mortal we have ever in this world fallen in with; sadder even than poetic Dante. His is a *no*god-like sorrow; sadder than the godlike. The Chartist editor, dull as he, calls him demon author. and a man set on by the Poor-Law Commissioners. What a black, godless, waste-struggling world, in this once merry England of ours, do such pamphlets and such editors betoken! *Laissez-faire* and Malthus, Malthus and *Laissez-faire:* ought not *these* two at length to part company? Might we not hope that both of them had as good as delivered their message now, and were about to go their ways?

For all this of the 'painless extinction,' and the rest, is in a world where Canadian Forests stand unfelled, boundless Plains and Prairies unbroken with the plough; on the west and on the east, green desert spaces never yet made white with corn; and to the overcrowded little western nook of Europe, our Terrestrial Planet, nine-tenths of it yet vacant or tenanted by nomades, is still crying, Come and till me, come and reap me! And in an England with wealth, and means for moving, such as no nation ever before had. With ships; with war-ships rotting idle, which, but bidden move and not rot, might bridge all oceans. With trained men, educated to pen and practise, to administer and act; briefless Barristers, chargeless Clergy, taskless Scholars, languishing in all courthouses, hiding in obscure garrets, besieging all antechambers, in passionate want of simply one thing, Work;—with as many Half-pay Officers of both Services, wearing themselves down in wretched tedium, as might lead an Emigrant host larger than

Xerxes' was! *Laissez-faire* and Malthus positively must part company. Is it not as if this swelling, simmering, never-resting Europe of ours stood, once more, on the verge of an expansion without parallel; struggling, struggling like a mighty tree again about to burst in the embrace of summer, and shoot forth broad frondent boughs which would fill the whole earth? A disease; but the noblest of all,—as of her who is in pain and sore travail, but travails that she may be a mother, and say, Behold, there is a new Man born!

'True thou Gold-Hofrath,' exclaims an eloquent satirical German of our acquaintance, in that strange Book of his,[2] 'True thou Gold-Hofrath: too crowded indeed! Meanwhile what portion of this inconsiderable Terraqueous Globe have ye actually tilled and delved, till it will grow no more? How thick stands your population in the Pampas and Savannas of America; round ancient Carthage, and in the interior of Africa; on both slopes of the Altaic chain, in the central Platform of Asia; in Spain, Greece, Turkey, Crim Tartary, the Curragh of Kildare? One man, in one year, as I have understood it, if you lend him earth, will feed himself and nine others. Alas, where now are the Hengsts and Alarics of our still glowing, still expanding Europe; who, when their home is grown too narrow, will enlist and, like fire-pillars, guide onwards those superfluous masses of indomitable living Valour; equipped, not now with the battle-axe and war-chariot, but with the steamengine and ploughshare? Where are they?—Preserving their Game!'

---

[2]Sartor Resartus, p. 239.

Printed in Great Britain
by Amazon